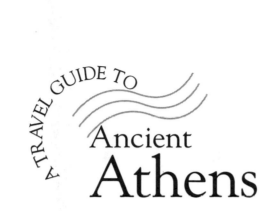

A TRAVEL GUIDE TO

Ancient
Athens

Other books in the Travel Guide series:

Ancient Alexandria
Ancient Rome
California Gold Country
Renaissance Florence
Shakespeare's London

A TRAVEL GUIDE TO

Ancient
Athens

Don Nardo

**LUCENT
BOOKS**

THOMSON
™
GALE

San Diego • Detroit • New York • San Francisco • Cleveland • New Haven, Conn. • Waterville, Maine • London • Munich

LIBRARY OF CONGRESS CATALOGING-IN-PUBLICATION DATA

Nardo, Don, 1947–
   Ancient Athens / By Don Nardo.
     p. cm. — (A Travel guide to:)
Summary: A historical look at ancient Athens and its people, education, weather,
transportation, hotels, shopping, festivals, sporting events, banks, government, and
sightseeing.
Includes bibliographical references and index.
  ISBN 1-59018-016-X
  1. Athens (Greece)—Guidebooks—Juvenile literature. 2. Athens (Greece)—History—
Juvenile literature. [1. Athens (Greece)—Civilization. 2. Greece—Civilization—To 146 B.C.]
I. Title. II. Series.
  DF289 .N37 2003
  914.95'120476—dc21

                                                   2002004893

Printed in the United States of America

Contents

FOREWORD   6

INTRODUCTION
A Note to the Reader   8

CHAPTER ONE
A Brief History of Athens   10

CHAPTER TWO
Weather and Physical Setting   18

CHAPTER THREE
Transportation, Lodging, and Food   24

CHAPTER FOUR
Shopping   34

CHAPTER FIVE
Athenian Government   42

CHAPTER SIX
Religious Worship and Festivals   51

CHAPTER SEVEN
Athletics and Recreation   62

CHAPTER EIGHT
Sightseeing in Athens   72

CHAPTER NINE
Daytrips to Nearby Sites   85

Notes   96
For Further Reading   98
Major Works Consulted   100
Additional Works Consulted   104
Index   106
Picture Credits   111
About the Author   112

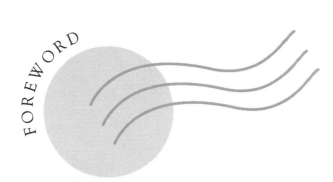

Travel can be a unique way to learn about oneself and other cultures. The esteemed American writer and historian, John Hope Franklin, poetically expressed his conviction in the value of travel by urging, "We must go beyond textbooks, go out into the bypaths and untrodden depths of the wilderness and travel and explore and tell the world the glories of our journey." The message communicated by this eloquent entreaty is clear: The value of travel is to temper one's imagination about a place and its people with reality, and instead of thinking how things may be, to be able to experience them as they really are.

Franklin's voice is not alone in his summons for students to "travel and explore." He is joined by a stentorian chorus of thinkers that includes former president John F. Kennedy, who established the Peace Corps to facilitate cross-cultural understandings between Americans and citizens of other lands. Ideas about the benefits of travel do not spring only from contemporary times. The ancient Greek historian, Herodotus journeyed to foreign lands for the purpose of immersing himself in unfamiliar cultural traditions. In this way, he believed, he might gain a first-hand understanding of people and ways of life in other places.

The joys, insights, and satisfaction that travelers derive from their journeys are not limited to cultural understanding. Travel has the added value of enhancing the traveler's inner self by expanding his or her range of experiences. Writer Paul Tournier concurs that, "The real meaning of travel, like that of a conversation by the fireside, is the discovery of oneself through contact with other people."

The Lucent Books' Travel Guide series enlivens history by introducing a new and innovative style and format. Each volume in the series presents the history of a preeminent historical travel destination written in the casual style and format of a travel guide. Whether providing a tour of fifth-century Athens, Renaissance Florence, or Shakespeare's London, each book describes a city or area at its cultural peak and orients readers to only those places and activities that are known to have existed at that time.

A high level of authenticity is achieved in the Travel Guide series. Each book is written in the present tense and addresses the reader as a prospective foreign traveler. The sense of authenticity if further achieved, whenever possible, by the inclusion of descriptive quotations by contemporary writers who knew the place; information on fascinating historical sites; and travel tips meant to explain unusual cultural idiosyncrasies that give depth and texture to all great cultural centers. Even shopping details, such as where to buy an ermine trimmed gown, or a much needed house slave are included to inform readers of what items were sought after throughout history.

Looked at collectively, this series presents an appealing presentation of many of the cultural and social highlights of Western civilization. The collection also provides a framework for discussion about the larger historical currents that dominated not only each travel destination but countries and entire continents as well. Each book is customized by the author to bring to the fore the most important and most interesting characteristics that define each title. High standards of scholarship are assured in the series by the generous peppering of relevant quotes and extensive bibliographies. These tools provide readers a scholastic standard for their own research as well as a guide to direct them to other books, periodicals, and websites that will provide them greater breadth and detail.

A Note to the Reader

This book examines known facts about the ancient Greeks, particularly the Athenians and their history and culture, in the format of a modern-style travel guide. Such an approach provides an innovative and entertaining way to learn about ancient Greek life and ideas. At the same time, however, it presents some technical problems that do not exist in straightforward history texts.

At issue, for example, are conventions of dating. The B.C.-A.D. dating system in common use today did not exist in ancient times. But for the sake of clarity and convenience, this book uses that system.

As for the dating of the travel guide itself, the author has chosen the year 340 B.C. for some important reasons. First, it was near the end of the Classical Age, which modern scholars date from circa 500 B.C. to 323 B.C. It was during the Classical Age that Athens defeated the Persians, built a maritime empire, expanded its democracy, erected the Parthenon and other immortal temples atop its Acropolis, and in general reached its height of power and influence. Only after most of these events had come to pass did the city attract large numbers of tourists, traders, and other travelers from all across the Greek world and beyond. The chosen date of 340 B.C. is also crucial because it is only two years before Athens, its image, and its independent status underwent some significant changes. In 338 B.C. Philip II, king of Macedonia, defeated Athens and the other major city-states and seized the hegemony (political and military dominance) of Greece. After that, Athens was never quite the same. Thus, this travel guide describes the city when it was still a major political power, as well as a potent cultural model, in Greece.

Just as the Greeks had their own dating systems, they also had their own units of measurement. But as in the case of dates, this book employs modern units of measurement—miles and square miles—as well as degrees of temperature and so forth, to make the text more understandable to modern readers. Except for these conventions, all aspects of this travel guide are authentic. They are based on evidence derived from surviving ancient literary texts and studies made by archaeologists and other scholars of paintings, sculptures, buildings, tools, weapons, coins, and other ancient artifacts. All of the places and sights described are or were real; many still exist in modern Athens and its environs, although they are now in a ruined state.

CHAPTER ONE

A Brief History of Athens

Visitors to Athens often marvel at the fact that almost everywhere they tread they seem to step on or over some relic of history. This is hardly an exaggeration, for the city is one of the oldest in Greece; and the local inhabitants claim a proud historical tradition stretching back to the Age of Heroes.[1]

Today, in the year 340 B.C., as this new travel guide is being compiled, Athens is Greece's most popular tourist attraction by far. And without a doubt, a majority of visitors come to see its many historical sights and artifacts. For that reason, therefore, a brief overview of the city's history is in order.

Every year thousands of travelers come from all parts of the Mediterranean world to see the wonders of Athens, including its magnificent Acropolis complex.

Athens in Heroic Times

Long ago, according to legend, Athena, goddess of war and wisdom, and the sea god Poseidon had a contest to decide which of them would preside over and protect Athens. Poseidon touched the Acropolis (the renowned rocky hill in the city's center) with his trident, producing a miraculous saltwater spring. Then Athena caused the first olive tree to sprout from the hill's summit. Seeing this, Zeus and the other gods judging the contest declared her the winner. (Another version of the story says a mortal, King Cecrops, judged the contest.) Ever since that time, Athena has been the city's divine patron, protecting it on numerous occasions.

In those days the urban center of Athens was only one, though the largest, of the many scattered towns and villages of Attica (the territory controlled by Athens). Sometime in the Age of Heroes, the great Athenian champion Theseus unified them all into a single political unit. He also defended the city itself against an attack by the Amazons, the fabulous tribe of warrior women said to inhabit the wild lands northwest of the Black Sea. Later in the age, Athens was among the Greek kingdoms that assembled to attack Troy (after a Trojan prince, Paris, abducted the beautiful Helen, queen of Sparta). In the famous catalog of combatants in his *Iliad*, Homer says the Athenians contributed fifty ships to the expedition.

Athena's Miraculous Birth

The goddess Athena, who figures so prominently in Athens's history and folklore, is said to have had quite an unusual birth. According to tradition, she sprang, fully clad in her armor, from the head of her father, Zeus. The seventh-century B.C. *Greek poet Hesiod recorded the details of this miraculous event in his* Theogony:

Zeus first took the goddess Metis [a deity known for her great wisdom] as his wife, but later deceived her and swallowed her, for fate had decreed that Metis would conceive children filled with wisdom. And the first of these would be the bright-eyed maiden Athena, who would have strength and wisdom equal to her father's. Metis remained concealed inside of Zeus and eventually conceived Athena, who received from her father the *aegis* [his majestic and invincible breastplate], with which she surpassed in strength all her brother and sister gods. And Zeus brought her into the world, bearing the *aegis* and clad in battle armor, from out of his head.

The Poet

No Greek city's history, including that of Athens, can ignore the events described by Homer in his epic poems, the *Iliad* and the *Odyssey*. For the benefit of non-Greeks, Homer is the greatest writer Greece has ever produced, and Greeks everywhere refer to him simply and reverently as "the Poet." His birthplace is disputed, with several cities in Greek Ionia claiming him, though Chios is the most plausible candidate. The first known written editions of his epics were those commissioned by the Athenian leader Pisistratus in the mid–sixth century B.C. Since that time, these works have come to exert a profound influence on Greek culture and thought. The *Iliad*, describing a series of incidents near the end of the Trojan War, and the *Odyssey*, telling the adventures of Odysseus—one of the Greek kings who fought at Troy—are major sources of information about the Greek gods, their powers, habits, and wrath. In addition, Homer's epics have provided the Greeks with a blueprint for a heroic, noble code of conduct. They contain numerous examples of practical wisdom, remain the primary literary texts studied by Greek schoolchildren, and are endlessly quoted by Greek writers of all kinds.

The Growth of Democracy

After the close of the Age of Heroes, Athens remained a prominent city. Over the course of many years—just how many no one can say—the Athenians eliminated their kingship and began instituting the more democratic institutions for which the city has become deservedly famous. In this course of events, the common people increasingly came to resent the monopoly the nobles held on government and public affairs. Some of the commoners got together from time to time in a meeting called the Assembly (Ecclesia); but this group had no real say in government. The people also complained that there was no written law code, so that justice was often dispensed in an arbitrary and unfair way. In an attempt to conciliate the commoners, the nobles appointed one of their own men, Draco, to draft a written law code. His laws were seen as much too harsh, however, and the city soon tottered on the brink of a bloody social revolution.

In a last-ditch effort to avoid civil war, in 594 B.C. the opposing groups asked Solon, a citizen with a reputation for wisdom and fairness, to intercede. He eliminated Draco's repressive laws (except for those dealing with murder). He also introduced a new social ranking based on wealth rather than birth, which made it possible for commoners to rise to the rank of archon (chief administrator). And he created the Council (Boule), a group of four hundred men chosen by lot from all classes; they prepared the agenda for the Assembly and served to balance the power of the aristocrats.

It was only a matter of time before these changes led to full-blown democracy. About eighty-six years after Solon's reforms (roughly 508 B.C.), a leading aristocrat named Cleisthenes saw the wisdom of offering the commoners more of a say in government in return for their support. According to the Athenian historian Herodotus, Cleisthenes "took the [common] people into his party,"[2] by increasing the powers of the Assembly and reducing the authority wielded by the aristocrats. The new system, with its thorough mix of people from all social classes, operated

Athens contributed fifty ships to the great expedition to Troy. Here we see the Greeks climbing from their hiding place inside the Trojan Horse.

(and still operates) on the principle of equality under the law (known as *isonomia*).

Athens on the Anvil of War

Not long after the Athenians created their democracy (Greece's first and, to this writer's knowledge, the first in the known world), they were sorely tested on the anvil of war. In 490 B.C. the Persian king Darius I sent an army to conquer Athens; and the Athenians met and defeated these barbarians on the Plain of Marathon, in northeastern Attica. Athens also played a pivotal role in driving out the invasion forces of Darius's son, Xerxes, ten years later. The great Greek naval victory at Salamis, fought only a few miles west of Athens's urban center, was largely engineered by the Athenian leader Themistocles.

After the defeat of the Persians, Athens had the most powerful navy and was the most prosperous and prestigious

The great Solon dictates his famous laws to some young scribes. Thanks to Solon, the seeds of democracy took strong root in Athens and have since produced impressive fruits.

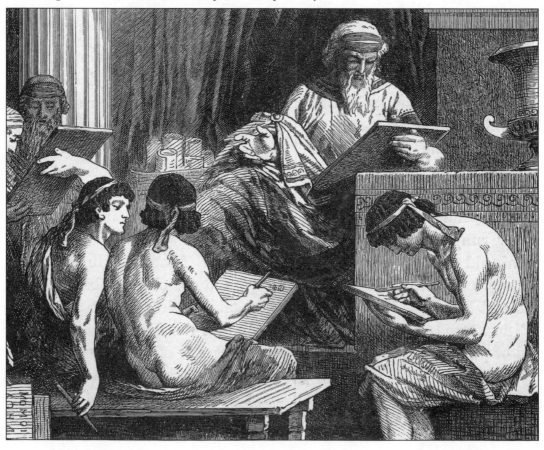

Pericles delivers his renowned funeral oration over the first Athenians who gave their lives in the great war against Sparta and its allies.

state in Greece. And the Athenian leaders Cimon and Pericles took advantage of these strengths by rapidly building up a maritime empire. At its height, more than one hundred Greek cities came under Athens's economic and political influence. (Much of the money the city accumulated in these years went into the creation of the marvelous monuments on the Acropolis, which Pericles oversaw and which today remain the chief attractions to visitors from far and wide.)

Meanwhile, the city's rival—Sparta, in the Peloponnesus (the large peninsula making up southern Greece)—was not pleased. At the time the Spartans were renowned for having the best land army in Greece. And the two states bickered and fought off and on for a number of years. Finally, they and their respective groups of allies clashed in the dreadful Peloponnesian War. Athens lost, but fortunately it managed to recover in only a few short years. In 371 B.C. the Athenians were gladdened to see the Spartans humbled by the Theban general Epaminondas, who crushed their army at Leuctra (in the region of Boeotia, north of Attica). And Sparta

Athens's Greatest Orator

Demosthenes is Athens's most accomplished and respected orator; some say he is the greatest Greek orator of all times. He began his career writing court speeches and eventually began speaking in Athens's Assembly, where his oratorical skills were immediately evident. In 351 B.C. the patriotic Demosthenes became distressed when Macedonia's new king, Philip II, began his campaigns of expansion in northern Greece. That year the orator delivered his *First Philippic*, calling on his countrymen to recapture the northern Aegean city of Amphipolis, which Philip had recently taken. Two years later, responding to Philip's siege of the city of Olynthus, Demosthenes attacked Philip again in a series of speeches known as the *Olynthiacs*. But most Greeks ignored these pleas. Soon afterward (in 346 B.C.), Demosthenes and his fellow orator Aeschines went to Macedonia to negotiate a peace settlement; but this came to nothing thanks to Philip's subsequent aggressions. These events also marked the beginning of a bitter rivalry between the two orators, with Demosthenes accusing Aeschines of taking bribes from Philip. Aeschines continues strenuously to deny this charge.

Always in the forefront of political affairs, Demosthenes has a reputation for honesty and frankness.

has posed no threat to Athens or any other Greek state since that time.

The Present International Situation

Today Athens and its neighbors worry about a much more formidable threat than Sparta ever was. I speak of the Macedonians, those barbaric Greek-speakers from the far north. In the past few years, their king, Philip II, has attacked and captured one Greek city after another. Just six years ago, two highly respected Athenian orators, Demosthenes and Aeschines, went to Macedonia hoping to negotiate a peace settlement. But their efforts were in vain. In that same year, the slippery Philip, while claiming he had no thirst for conquest, marched his army right into southern Greece. At this writing, the Macedonians are more or less inactive. But Demosthenes fears that Philip is only biding his time and therefore remains an insidious threat. "One day Philip's policy will cause you more distress than it does now," the orator declared in a recent speech to the Athenian Assembly, "for I see the plot thickening. I hope I may prove a false prophet, but I fear the catastrophe is even now only too near. So when you can no longer shut your eyes to what is happening . . . then I expect that you will be angry and exasperated."[3]

To be on the safe side, the Assembly has authorized a sharp increase in shipbuilding and other naval preparedness. Decent, civilized Greeks everywhere hope and pray that these precautions will be all that is needed, that Philip will take his ruffians and go back to the uncultured backwater he calls home. The visitor who questions Athenians on the street will find them somewhat worried but resolute. All insist that they will fight, if necessary, to preserve the monuments, traditions, and freedoms that make Athens the marvel and envy of this or any age. (In the unlikely event that war does break out in the foreseeable future, foreign visitors wishing to return to their home cities should not use land routes, as these will likely be unsafe. Instead, they should make their way to Athens's port town—Piraeus—and book passage on whatever cargo ships and other private crafts are available. Philip has no navy to speak of and poses no threat to Athenian naval supremacy.)

CHAPTER TWO

Weather and Physical Setting

Visitors to Athens who hail from cities along the coastal regions of the Greek mainland, Aegean Islands, and coastal Ionia,[4] will find the local climate quite familiar. Like these and other Mediterranean shores, Athens has what some have termed "Mediterranean" weather, characterized by long, hot, dry summers and relatively short, cool, damp winters. The average warmth at sea level in Hekatombaion (July) is about 81°F, enough to make a person break into a sweat without much exertion. And even in winter there are many bright and sunny, if not always warm, days. Only as one climbs high onto Mount Pentelikon and some of the other peaks that rise in central Attica does the air get noticeably cooler in the summer months.

The first and perhaps most obvious way that this generally amenable climate has affected Athenian life is by drawing people outdoors. The city's Assembly meetings, public sacrifices, theatrical per-formances, and other such events are held in the open air. And like most other Greeks, male Athenians tend to view their houses as simple places for sleeping and other necessary personal activities; they prefer outdoor group settings, such as the marketplace, street corners, gymnasia practice fields, and so on. The local climate obviously also plays a key role in planning such activities as planting crops, herding animals overland, holding religious festivals, and moving troops and fighting battles in wartime.

Attica and Its Terrain

As for Athens's general physical setting, Attica is a roughly triangular-shaped peninsula jutting downward from the southeastern sector of the Greek mainland into the Aegean's sparkling blue waters. The peninsula is very extensive—covering about 965 square miles.[5] That makes Athens unusually large for a Greek state. And this has proved highly advantageous over the years for the Athenian people. On the one hand, it has allowed them enough space to raise a large, diversified population; on the other, it has provided them plentiful quantities of certain important natural resources, notably clay and marble. The clay has made possible the production of the city's highly valued pottery, used throughout the eastern Mediterranean sphere. And the marble has been used for the construction of the magnificent stone temples that attract so many foreign tourists each year.

These advantages aside, at first glance Attica might seem an unlikely place to build a splendid, influential culture. Beside the fact that the peninsula is located in the driest part of Greece, its terrain is mostly rocky and rugged, and its soil mostly thin. The noted Athenian scholar

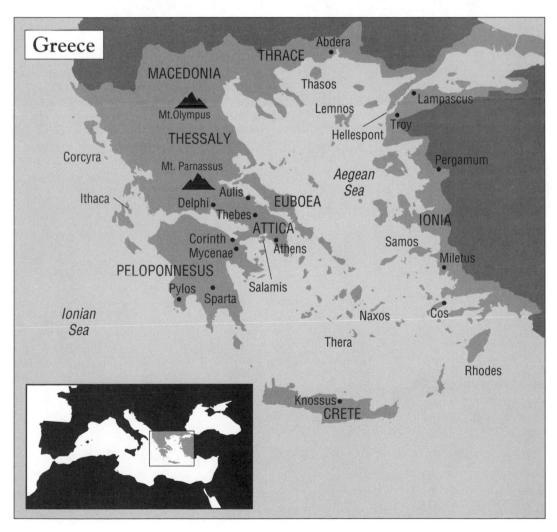

Plato, who died seven years before this writing, at age eighty, left behind this fitting description:

> The whole country is only a long promontory [peninsula] extending far into the sea away from the rest of the continent [Greek mainland], while the surrounding basin of the sea is everywhere deep in the neighborhood of the shore. . . . There has never been any considerable accumulation of the soil coming down from the mountains, as in other places, but the earth [good soil] has fallen away all round and sunk out of sight. The consequence is that . . . there are remaining only the bones of the wasted body, as they may be called . . . all the richer and softer parts of the soil having fallen away, and the mere skeleton of the land being left.[6]

Indeed, because it lacks enough good soil, Attica produces only about a quarter of the grain consumed yearly by Athens's

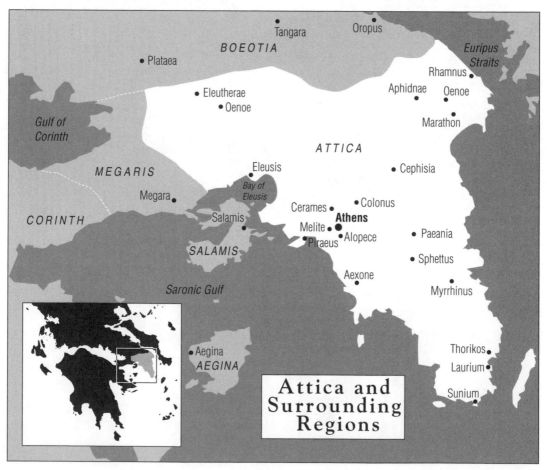

Attica and Surrounding Regions

Merchant vessels crowd the main harbor at Piraeus, Athens's port city. Many travelers disembark at Piraeus and walk inland to the Athenian urban center.

population of over three hundred thousand people. The rest has to be imported from foreign states, mostly located on the more fertile shores of the Black Sea. (It was Sparta's capture of Athens's life-giving grain route that brought about the Spartan victory in the Peloponnesian War.)

Nevertheless, Attica has a number of scattered cool springs and shady groves of elms and cypresses. And some crops—chief among them olives, figs, and grapes—thrive in the local climate and soil. Moreover, the Athenian state is situated in a geographically strategic position, allowing it easy access to a majority of the important mainland and Aegean city-states, which is a boon to trade. From the port of Piraeus, on the Saronic Gulf about five miles southwest of the main town, Athenian merchant vessels venture far and wide, trading a wide variety of goods.

The Urban Center

Within Athens's urban center itself, the most strategic spot is and always has been the Acropolis. Rising nearly four hundred feet from the surrounding plain, this huge, rugged limestone rock constitutes a natural fortress and has become the focus of the city's major religious worship and tourist trade. Two other, smaller rocky outcrops—the Areopagus ("Hill of Ares," site of a major law court) and the Pnyx Hill (where the Assembly meets)—rise to the west of the Acropolis.

This drawing shows Athens's Agora from the west. The Thriasian Gate is visible at far left and the Acropolis rises in the distance at far right.

Piraeus's Orderly Layout

Visitors to Attica are often struck by the contrasting layouts of Athens's urban center and its port of Piraeus. The streets of the urban center wind to and fro in a chaotic jumble, while those in the port form a neat, orderly, and convenient grid. The reason for this disparity is that Athens is very ancient, with streets conforming to old goat and sheep paths and the like; whereas Piraeus is comparatively new and therefore bears the imprint of modern city planning. The government abandoned the old port on Phaleron Bay only about a century and a half ago and replaced it with the new port on the neighboring promontory of Akte. Of the three harbors at Akte, the largest—Kantharos—became the principal anchorage for trading ships. The smaller harbors of Sdea and Mounykhia, farther east, are devoted to warships. Eventually, the archons hired a city planner named Hippodamus, a native of Miletus; and he laid out Piraeus's streets in their grid pattern, following those of Miletus and several other Ionian Greek cities.

Meanwhile, a brook, the Eridanos, flows about half a mile to the north of the Acropolis, roughly marking the northern border of the Agora, where the city's government buildings and marketplace are situated. Athens's main entranceway, the Thriasian Gate,[7] through which a majority of travelers enter, lies just to the northwest of the Agora; so the busy marketplace forms the initial and usually a favorable impression for first-time visitors to the city.

Transportation, Lodging, and Food

The means one chooses for traveling to Athens will depend largely on one's starting point. For those who live along the coasts of the Greek mainland, Aegean Islands, Ionia, and of course more distant foreign lands, a ship is by far the best choice. On the one hand, sea travel is faster, more convenient, and considerably less strenuous than going by land; on the other, it is usually more pleasant. The docks at Piraeus are large and can accommodate many ships. And the walk from

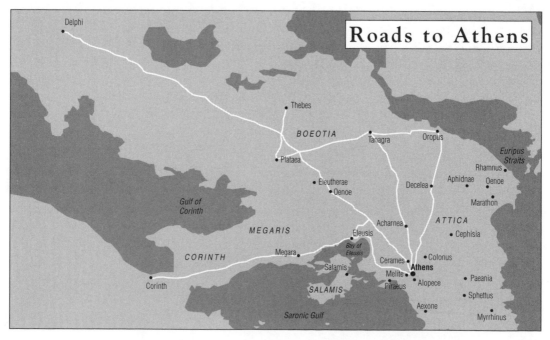

Roads to Athens

Delphi

Thebes

BOEOTIA

Tanagra

Oropus

Euripus
Straits

Plataea

Rhamnus

Eleutherae
Oenoe

Decelea

Aphidnae
Oenoe

Gulf of
Corinth

Marathon

ATTICA

Acharnea

Cephisia

MEGARIS

Eleusis

Bay of
Eleusis

Megara

Cerames

Colonus

CORINTH

Salamis

Melite
Piraeus

Athens

Alopece

Paeania

Corinth

SALAMIS

Aexone

Sphettus

Saronic Gulf

Myrrhinus

Trouble on the Roads

Most Greek roads are so narrow that two wagons approaching each other from opposite directions cannot pass at the same time. One vehicle must pull off the road to accommodate the other; and sometimes this leads to trouble. Perhaps the most famous incident of this type was the legendary encounter between the old Theban king Laius and a Corinthian traveler named Oedipus (who turned out to be Laius's son, though neither knew it at the time). The Athenian playwright Sophocles captured the moment in his great play Oedipus the King, *in which years later Oedipus tells his wife:*

I came near to a triple crossroads and there I was met by a herald and a man riding on a horse-drawn wagon. . . . The driver, and the old man himself, tried to push me off the road. In anger, I struck the driver, who was shoving me. When the old man saw me coming, he grasped his water jug, aimed at my head, and hit me. But I paid him back in full. I struck him with my walking stick, knocking him backwards out of the wagon. Then I killed the whole lot of them.

Piraeus to Athens's urban center takes only a little over an hour (except in inclement weather).

However, most people living in the inland regions of the mainland have little other choice than to take the roads. Walking is the most common mode of travel; but some people prefer to ride in carts or wagons, or at least to carry their belongings or wares in them. Those attempting the journey to Athens are advised to make their way to one of the main routes and stick to it. There are two main reasons for doing so. First, these roads are well traveled and one is less likely to meet up with robbers on them than on the more remote mountain paths. Second, some of the main roads (those connecting the main cities with major religious sites) have been provided with artificial ruts to accommodate the wheels of carts and wagons. (Keep in mind that these are designed for standard vehicles, with wheels nine or fewer inches wide and fifty-seven inches apart; people with nonstandard carts should leave them at home and opt for donkeys or mules to carry their belongings.)

The main rutted roads leading to Athens are as follows. The longest and best begins at Apollo's sacred sanctuary at Delphi and winds southeastward through Boeotia, passing close to Thebes. Travelers from Epirus, Acarnania, Aetolia, Thessaly, Trachis, Doris, and other points north and west of Delphi should take local roads that lead to the Delphi-Athens rutted road. Only parts of the main road leading out of the Peloponnesus (a route that passes through the Isthmus of Corinth and joins with the Delphi-Athens road) are rutted;

however, the other sections are well kept, as this road bears heavy traffic from the spring through fall seasons. The most difficult and dangerous section of this road is the six-mile stretch that skirts the upper edge of the Saronic Gulf, southwest of Megara; it follows the edge of some steep cliffs and is very narrow in places.

Within Attica itself, a rutted road connects Eleusis and Athens (a distance of twelve miles); and a partially rutted road leads northward from Athens, passes through the villages of Decelea (in central Attica) and Oropus (in northern Attica), then turns westward into Boeotia, reaching Tanagra, Plataea, and eventually seven-gated Thebes. Take note that this road has a toll station in the busy summer season, although the toll is minimal and collected only from those entering Attica. Residents of northern and eastern Attica usually take local paths to the fourteen-mile stretch of road connecting Mount Pentelikon to Athens. This was the route over which Pericles' workmen carried the stones for the great Acropolis complex. To carry their tremendous weight, the road was paved with stone slabs, and it features a double set of carved ruts to accommodate two-way wagon traffic. Many call it the best road in all of Greece.

The Risk of Robbery

Apart from these and the other main routes, most of the roads in mainland Greece are mere paths. They should be avoided by long-distance travelers, partly because they are often rocky, muddy, and impassable when it rains, and remote, making them favorite haunts for highwaymen. Regarding the latter, it is best not to journey along any mainland roads carrying large amounts of gold and silver coins and other valuables. Many people have made the mistake of doing so and lost their life savings to robbers. A safe alternative is to leave most of one's coins, jewelry, and so forth in a temple treasury (or with a banker) for safekeeping and carry only the bare minimum needed for paying one's way. That way if a man is unfortunate enough to be accosted by robbers, he will still have resources.

Anyone who *has* been robbed on his way to Athens has rather limited, though sometimes promising, options. On reaching the urban center, he should first seek out his local *proxenos,* if any. (For non-Greeks, a *proxenos* is a resident—either a citizen or resident alien—of a Greek city who takes care of the interests of the people of another city. At present, for example, Demosthenes is the Athenian *proxenos* for Thebes and its citizens. He gives Thebans visiting Athens legal, financial, and other advice; helps them find lodgings; gets them good seats at the theater; and so on.) In many cases, the *proxenos* for the traveler's city will be glad to loan him the money he needs for his stay in Athens. (The traveler is expected to repay his benefactor later, of course.)

Another, less certain alternative for the destitute traveler is to make the rounds of local bankers (*trapezitai*). Some have been known to lend such people money;

however, they charge very high interest rates (from 10 to 30 percent, as compared to zero interest charged by one's *proxenos*). For those happy few who can afford it, one way of avoiding being robbed in the first place is to take a gang of slaves along on the journey for protection.

Finding a Place to Stay

Those visitors to Athens who have established family or friendship ties with local citizens naturally do not have to worry about finding lodging. The larger family homes almost always have a guest room (*xenon*), often with its own entrance. Businesses that deal on a regular basis with traders from var-

ious cities also routinely provide small but adequate accommodations for visitors. In addition, a number of smaller Athenian homes welcome strangers to stay with them. (As part of the ancient custom of *xenia*—two-way hospitality—these hosts can then expect to have a place to stay when they visit their guest's home city.) In all such arrangements, by tradition the host invites the guest to dinner on his first night in town, after which the traveler must fend for himself. (An exception is a close family member or friend, who may end up eating all his or her meals in the host's dining room.) On departure the guest and host exchange gifts.

This is the front façade of the house of a wealthy Athenian businessman. He is known for his hospitality and offers two guest rooms to visitors from other cities.

Visitors who have no family, friends, or business associates in Athens must seek other kinds of lodging. The most common alternative is a room at an inn (*pandokeion*). Several private inns exist along the main roads coming into the urban center, as well as in both downtown Athens and the port of Piraeus. Some are run by local temples and some are privately run. In general, those outside the city are larger, though not necessarily more comfortable. The country inns tend to follow the plan of the one at the Temple of Hera outside Athens's neighbor—Plataea. The place is a big rectangle about two hundred feet on a side, with a huge inner courtyard.

Lining the courtyard are 150 rooms on two levels, with a roofed walkway running in front of each row of rooms. The inns in Athens and Piraeus look similar, but are much smaller and offer fewer rooms.

Travelers should be warned that most of the rooms in these inns are quite small and cramped. Also, because of high demand, especially during the Panathenaea, the guest staying in a city inn may have to share a room with one, two, or even three other travelers. Average-quality inns supply wooden cots, on which the guest can place his bedroll, and a small table; while the cheaper establishments offer only straw-filled mattress-

The inn on the road to Eleusis is known for its clean rooms and friendly host. Travelers carrying valuables can leave them for safekeeping in the small treasury across the road.

Herms Here, There, and Everywhere

Non-Greeks are often perplexed and fascinated by piles of small stones, large upright stones, and occasionally rough-cut statues that appear in large numbers along Greek roadways everywhere, including those leading to and from Athens. All of these are *hermeia*, shrines to the messenger god Hermes, who is also the patron of travelers. By custom, people on long trips place an extra stone on a heap, which as a consequence gets increasingly larger. The sculpted versions are usually set up by well-to-do citizens hoping to appease the god. Greek travelers often carry small flasks of olive oil, which they pour onto the herms as a liquid offering.

More realistic-looking Herms are set up outside most homes to keep evil from entering. This one guards the front of a country house not far from Athens's urban center.

es on the floor. Rooms in a majority of inns tend to be dark, as few have windows. Only a few innkeepers supply candles or oil lamps, so travelers should carry one or the other (and preferably both) in their luggage. There are no toilets in such rooms, either. Instead, guests are supplied with chamber pots, which are emptied by servants daily in the better inns, but less frequently in the seedier places.

Those wishing to bathe must go out to the nearest bathhouse, of which several can be found in Athens. Bathhouses are generally small establishments, each equipped with a changing room and a washing room. Patrons are advised to have a friend or slave watch their clothes and personal belongings while in the washroom, as the management typically takes no responsibility for stolen items. The bathhouse usually supplies a small pot of lime, wood ashes, or fuller's earth to use as soap; but the guest is expected to supply his own towel. After cleansing himself, he stands over a large basin and allows some slaves with water buckets to rinse him off.

Those visitors who lack both the connections needed to find a *xenon* and the money for an inn will have to resort to the loggias in the Agora. In the daytime these covered public walkways serve as refuges for citizens seeking to escape the hot noonday sun or a sudden downpour; at night poor travelers are allowed to camp in them.

Finding Food

As in other Greek cities, inns do not normally include food in the price for the room. But sometimes the visitor can bargain with the innkeeper and pay extra for kitchen privileges; that is, the guest can buy food at the market and cook it (or have a

A platter of fruit and cup of wine are hallmarks of Greek cuisine. These and other foods, including cheese and pastries, are available at any tavern in Athens.

servant cook it) in the inn's kitchen. In a similar vein, a guest staying in a *xenon* can sometimes work out a deal in advance for kitchen privileges in the host's home.

All others will need to eat out. Athens has many small taverns (*kapeleia*) that offer food and drink. (Some are mainly drinking establishments and provide only snacks, such as figs and cheese.) They are most numerous in the Agora, but quite a few can be found in other sections of town, as well as along the roadways leading into it. Taverns—which offer an informal, relaxed, often jovial setting for people of all walks of life—are so common and accepted in Athens that Diogenes the Cynic has remarked, "Taverns are the dining halls of Attica,"[8] a sarcastic comparison to the more formal, colorless communal dining halls in which Spartan men share their meals. (Those visitors to Athens who happen to meet up with or perhaps actually seek out Diogenes will find him a colorful, if not zany, fixture of Athenian life. He and his followers hold that happiness can only be achieved through the rejection of all luxury and personal possessions and by living on the barest of essentials. He often carries a lantern around in the daytime, claiming to be searching for an honest man. So far, he says, he has yet to find one. Because he sometimes quite unashamedly relieves himself in public, the locals call him "the dog." So perhaps he is not the best person to ask for advice about where to eat.)

The fare in Athens's taverns varies, depending on the size and quality of the

A Helpful Hint About Torches

Athenian taverns supply more than just food and drink. They also sell torches, which both local residents and foreign visitors find essential after the sun goes down. The city's streets are quite dark. The exceptions are cloudless nights when the moon is full and along stretches of the market areas, where residual light from the shops and taverns provides illumination. Without a torch, the walker runs a high risk of tripping over stones and curbs or twisting an ankle in a pothole or rut. A torch also allows a person to see what is happening above him. The unfortunate fact is that not everyone observes the friendly custom of yelling "Watch out below!" when emptying a chamber pot out the window.

establishment. The smaller ones feature some and the larger places many of the following items: bread, barley porridge, cakes and other pastries, cheese, yogurt, *maza* (a paste made from grain, lentils, or beans), fruit (including figs, dates, grapes, and currants), eggs, olives, vegetables (including beans, lentils, peas, lettuce, onions, beets, and mushrooms), fish and shellfish, fowl (including ducks, geese, pigeons, owls,

Athenians recline while drinking Chian wine. Wine produced on the isle of Chios is among the most expensive and highly sought-after wines in the Greek-speaking world.

larks, jays, and nightingales), and meat (including lamb, deer, boar, and rabbit).

Wines from Far and Wide

To wash down their food, patrons can find a wide variety of wines available in Athenian taverns. Most of the wine consumed in the city is made locally in Attica and is fairly undistinguished, as well as cheap. The Athenians generally refer to it as *trikotylos*, or "three-container" wine, because one can buy three half-pints of it for just one obol. It is not uncommon for members of the upper classes to look down on this kind of wine drinking—cheap and by the glass, that is—and by association to scorn the whole tavern scene as lowbrow. The well-to-do prefer their elegant after-dinner parties (symposia), held in their private homes, where they serve more expensive imported wines.

However, the typical tavern keeper (*kapelos*) carries the imports, too, even if only a minority of his customers can afford them. The best and by far the most expensive wine comes from the Aegean island of Chios, particularly the variety made in the northwestern region of the island—Ariusia. In the taverns, Chian wine sells for three or four times the cost of Attic wines. Athenian taverns and wine merchants also carry other fine Greek wines, including those made in Mende, Samos, Lesbos, Thasos, and Magnesia. Many a bartender and wine merchant has been known to recite a line spoken by Dionysus, god of the vine, in a play by Hermippus (a writer popular in Pericles' time):

With Mendaean wine, the gods themselves wet their soft beds. And then there is Magnesian [wine], generous, sweet, and smooth, and Thasian, upon whose surface skates the perfume of apples; this I judge by far the best of all wines, except for blameless, painless Chian.[9]

The privilege of enjoying easy access to such a wide variety of wines from across the Greek world is one of the obvious benefits of Athens's wide-ranging trade network.

Following custom, most wines are mixed with water, a process that requires much skill lest the taste be ruined. And unfortunately, many *kapeloi* botch it, to the dismay of their customers. Plato and a number of other prominent Athenians have sung the praises of a *kapelos* named Sarambus, whose upscale tavern lies in the Agora. Sarambus is said to be the best wine mixer in Attica; and not surprisingly, the visitor will more often than not find his place crowded, with a line of would-be customers waiting outside the door. The same can be said for the tavern run by a Syracusan named Mithaecus, renowned as the best cook in Athens. The visitor might want to try the taverns run by Callias, Philo, or Agathon as alternatives. For those visiting Eleusis, in western Attica, the tavern of Aristander is well-known and highly recommended.

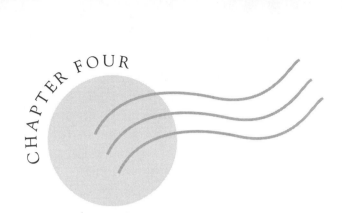

CHAPTER FOUR

Shopping

The Athenians like to brag that their city has the best shopping in the Greek world. This is largely a matter of opinion; however, no one can argue with the fact that Athens is a vast trade emporium, with an impressive array of goods from all parts of the known world. Athenian ships not only stop at Greek ports in the Aegean and Black Seas, southern Italy, and Sicily, but also barter

Athens's marketplace, the Agora, is by far the largest and busiest in the Greek world. All manner of trade goods from far and wide make their way here.

with Etruscans, Carthaginians, Egyptians, Arabs, Phoenicians, Syrians, Carians, Persians, and other non-Greeks. Only a partial list of Athenian imports includes: copper from the nearby island of Euboea; horses from Thessaly (in central Greece); wool and carpets from Miletus, Chios, and Samos (in Ionia); wine from Chios, Thasos, Mende, and other Aegean locations; metal figurines from Corinth and Argos (in the western Peloponnesus); fine linen and papyrus (for making writing parchment) from Egypt; frankincense and other spices from Syria; dates from Phoenicia; pork and fine aged cheeses from Syracuse (in Sicily); ivory from North Africa; animal hides from Gaul;[10] iron ore from the isle of Ilva[11] (off Italy's western coast); and wheat from the vast fields lying west and north of the Black Sea.

These and countless other goods make their way from the docks at Piraeus to shops both in that town and in Athens's urban center. Combined with the numerous foods, fabrics, clothes, shoes, vases, tableware, stone, bronze, and silver items, as well as other goods produced in Attica itself, they make shopping in Athens a convenient and fulfilling, if not exciting, experience.

Exchanging Money

Before making the rounds of the shops, however, the traveler needs to consider how he intends to pay for the goods they offer. Few Athenian merchants will barter goods for goods, as was common in ages past; instead, most demand currency, preferably gold or silver coins. If the visitor has Athenian silver drachmas (often called "owls" because they carry an image of Athena's sacred bird), his money is good anywhere in Attica. (In fact, his money is good almost anywhere in the Mediterranean, since owls are the most

These common coins issued by the Greek city of Syracuse are among the many foreign ones that visitors should exchange for Athenian silver drachmas (or "owls").

Athenian Money

Travelers need to be familiar with the Athenian monetary system, which is similar to the systems of some other Greek states, but quite different from foreign systems. The system is based on the drachma. The present standard drachma, the silver owl, weighs 4.31 grams. The main units of Athenian money break down as follows:

12 chalks = 1 obol
6 obols = 1 drachma
100 drachmas = 1 mina
60 minae (or 6,000 drachmas) = 1 talent

Note that minae and talents are represented by weights of silver rather than by coins. A talent, for instance, usually equals 57 pounds of silver. Some nonstandard but fairly common coins include the didrachm (equal to 2 drachmas), tetradrachm (4 drachmas), pentadrachm (5 drachmas), and diobol (2 obols).

common internationally accepted currency.) The same holds true if he possesses staters of electrum (a mixture of gold and silver) from Cyzicus (a prosperous Greek city lying just south of the entrance to the Black Sea); or Persian darics (valuable gold coins first issued by King Darius I).

Visitors with less-accepted local currencies, bronze ingots, jewelry, or other valuable goods will need to exchange them for acceptable coins. One alternative is to go to one of the few local temples that do such exchanges. The standard charge for doing the exchange is 6 percent. Much more plentiful are private bankers who act as money changers; indeed, they set up their tables outside temples and on practically every corner and square in the marketplace. (Non-Greeks take note that their title—*trapezitai*—translates literally as "table-men.") They

carefully weigh all coins and other valuables. And sometimes they scratch suspicious items with a piece of black jasper to make sure they are genuine. These men also charge 6 percent for exchanges; so it is probably best to exchange all of one's valuables at one time, to avoid multiple charges. (These bankers, as well as some temples, also extend loans, of course. But be warned that the interest on loans can sometimes be higher than 6 percent.)

Shopping in the Agora

Having secured the proper coinage, the visitor is ready to begin shopping. Although shops and vendors of various types can be found all over Athens, the vast majority are concentrated in the Agora, especially in the eastern sector, directly north of the Acropolis. One will find small shops there mixed in a jumble with private houses, taverns, inns, and other structures along narrow, winding streets. The average shop has one or two small rooms, one featuring a large opening in the front wall so that passersby can see some of the wares inside. A large number of merchants have more portable shops; each usually consists of a wagon filled with the vendor's goods and covered by awnings or in some cases a tent. They most often occupy a large open area in the central part of the Agora. A good many of these ven-dors are Attic farmers selling their fruits, vegetables, wines, birds, honey, hides, homespun, and other goods.

In a number of places, several merchants selling one kind of item have clustered together. So the Agora contains a so-called fish market (*ichthyopolisi*); a clothes market (*himatiopolis*); a women's market (*gynaikeia*, where one can find makeup, perfumes, homespun wool, and women's garments); and so forth. Specialized areas where furniture, slaves, and other household items are sold are

Slaves on sale in a specialized merchandise "ring" in the Agora. For the household, the most coveted and expensive slaves are those who have reading and writing skills.

Present Buying Power of the Drachma

How far will one's money go in Athens today? That is a burning question asked by most of the thousands of tourists who visit the city each year. To some degree, of course, prices are based on what local people can afford, which is tied to what they make. A rower in the Athenian navy, a bricklayer, and a carpenter all make roughly the same wage—2 drachmas per day, or about 600 or so drachmas per year. Skilled workers (sculptors, doctors, musicians, and so on) make two or three times that amount. A gallon of olive oil costs about 5 to 6 drachmas; a pair of shoes 8 to 12; a sheep about 12; a medium-priced slave 200 to 300 (or more if highly skilled); an acre of land 300 to 400; and a house in town 400 to 1,000, depending on its size and condition.

upper-class Athenian women are almost always escorted outside the home by a male slave or male family member; and any unaccompanied women seen wandering through the Agora are likely to be poor working women (who have no choice but to fend for themselves and their children) or prostitutes. Travelers from Sparta, Crete, and other regions where women have considerably more rights, freedom, and mobility often find Athenian social customs regarding women odd. Athenian men are very protective of their wives, daughters, sisters, and mothers. They restrict them to the home much of the time; make them stay in the "ladies' quarters," a room or rooms in the back of the house, when strange men are visiting; and keep a close eye on them in the few public gatherings that women are allowed to attend. Needless to say, to avoid trouble, perhaps even bodily harm, the visitor should avoid social contact with local women he encounters in the Agora and other public places (with the exception of prostitutes and female vendors or tavern keepers).

Shops of Local Artisans

Various goods and wares are also on sale in areas in which local artisans actually produce these items. One such area, which the Athenians call the Industrial District, is located just southeast of the Agora and north of the Areopagus hill. Here, the visitor will find shops where cobblers make and sell shoes and boots. One is run by the grandson of Simon, a close friend of the

often referred to collectively as *kykloi*, or "rings."

Strolling through the Agora's bustling, noisy maze of merchants and goods of every kind, the visitor will see Athenians of all walks of life. However, he will rarely see women shopping by themselves. Following polite custom, middle- and eccentric local gadfly, Socrates, and his protégé, Plato. However, the Industrial District is known more for its bronze- and marble-workers (*hermoglyphoi*). One can purchase small bronze or marble figurines, busts, and plaques, as well as life-size statues, in this area.

Farther north, beginning at Market Hill (on which the Temple of Hephaestos rests) and stretching nearly to the Thriasian Gate, is the Kerameikos, or "Potters' Quarter." Although the area is known for gambling and prostitution, it is also the traditional center of Athenian ceramics, widely considered among the finest in the world. Visitors have been known to stand for hours watching the potters ply their trade, employing techniques perfected

This old-style black-figured vase shows workers carrying and weighing bolts of cloth in a fabric shop. The Agora has many excellent fabric shops.

over many generations. The potters and their assistants mold wet clay (*ceramos*) on wheels and fire it in kilns reaching a temperature of a thousand degrees or more.

Though the Athenian master potters make vases, cups, jars, and other containers for practical use, they strive for originality of design and excellence of execution in every piece. The exquisite paintings that adorn these items come in various artistic styles. The most popular nowadays is the "red-figure" style, in which the figures of humans and animals are rendered in the fired pot's natural red-

dish tone and set against a black background. (This is a reversal of the "black-figure" decorative style that was very popular about a century and half ago; it featured figures painted black on the natural buff-colored background of a fired pot. The artist used a pointed tool to etch details into the figures.) In the red-figure technique, the painter applies details with a brush (although etching is still used on occasion). Another style originated by Athenian potters is the "white-ground" technique, in which the figures are painted in delicate lines against a white background. White-ground paint-

This is an example of a red-figure vase, the style most common today. Thousands of finely crafted examples are on sale in the Athenian Agora.

Metalsmiths at Work

The bronze work done in Athens's Industrial District ranks with the finest any-where in the known world. Visitors are sometimes allowed to watch the metal-smiths as they make figurines, bowls, and other items using various traditional cast-ing (molding) techniques. The simplest of these is to pour smelted bronze into a stone mold, allow it to dry, and then remove the mold. In another, the "lost-wax" method, a wax model is made of the object desired and then covered with clay. When fired in an oven, the clay hardens, but the wax melts away. The bronze is poured into the resulting hollow space, and when the metal solidifies, the clay is removed. A more complex method, called hollow-casting, allows the casting of larger, hollow bronze objects such as busts and statues (solid versions being too expensive and heavy). The metalworkers make a clay core, surround it with a wax model of the object desired, then cover the wax with more clay. When fired, the wax melts, leaving a hollow space with the dimensions and details of the original model. They then pour bronze into the hollow space and later remove the clay.

ings are most often used on funerary jars (*lekythoi*).

The prices of bronzes, marbles, ceram-ics, and other local Athenian wares vary considerably. Some artisans are more pop-ular and in demand than others, and the visitor is advised to check items for authen-ticity before buying them. Most Athenian artisans sign their works, but their signa-tures can be faked. So always make sure to purchase a work by a certain artisan only at his own shop.

CHAPTER FIVE

Athenian Government

All of the present democratic governments in Greek-speaking lands were either based directly on or inspired in large degree by Athens's democracy. So a good many of the city's yearly visitors take the time to inspect the complex of government buildings in the Agora and/or attend a meeting of the Assembly on the Pnyx Hill. Non-Greeks or residents of nondemocratic Greek states tend also to find the workings of Athenian democracy fascinating, if a bit alien or disturbing. Indeed, those who have grown up in more autocratic lands often fear that too much freedom is a dangerous thing. Plato himself warned his fellow Athenians that they must not allow their exceptional personal freedoms to lead them down the slippery slope to

disobedience to rulers; and then the attempt to escape control and advice of father, mother, elders, and . . . the controls of the laws also; and . . .

A Helpful Hint to Non-Greeks About the Demos

The term *demos* has other meanings besides the citizen body of a Greek city-state. It is sometimes used to denote the body of a city's poorer citizens, in contrast to the body of its wealthy and aristocratic ones. The term *demos* can also refer to the sum of a state's democratic laws and institutions; or to democrats, as opposed to people who are opposed to democracy; or in the case of Athens, to any local district, since Athenian districts, which the democratic reformer Cleisthenes set up, are called demes.

An Athenian citizen makes his case to the members of a jury. Athens's justice system is one of the most important cornerstones of its open democratic government.

the contempt of oaths and pledges, and no regard at all for the gods. . . . [We need to remind ourselves of this] from time to time . . . and then we shall not, as the proverb says, fall off our ass.[12]

The visitor will find, however, that most Athenians are not in the least worried about having too much freedom; in fact, they are renowned for their love of freedom, their open disdain for nondemocratic systems, and their boldness in promoting themselves and their own system and way of life. Unless the foreigner is not averse to loud and protracted arguments, therefore, he should try to avoid political discussions with the natives.

The Citizens and Their Assembly

Of Athens's numerous democratic institutions, the most fundamental is the Assembly, in which the citizen body (the *demos*) meets. In addition to directly electing some public officials, the Assembly has the sovereign authority to declare war, make peace, create commercial alliances, grant citizenship, found colonies, allocate public funds for construction and other projects, and decide foreign policy. The sweeping nature of its powers is best illustrated by its wartime responsibilities. The assembled citizens determine the overall strategy, how many soldiers or ships will be employed, and which generals will command. Those generals chosen then plan and carry out the specific battlefield strategies and tactics. No other citizen body in Greece (or the rest of the known world) has ever wielded so much direct authority in state affairs.

Only certain citizens, free males born in Attica, can take part in meetings of the Assembly. (Foreign visitors are usually welcome to watch but cannot participate in discussions or vote.) Male citizens are eligible for complete citizenship rights, including voting and holding public office, for which the minimum age is eighteen. Their female relatives are citizens, too, but a special type, the *astai*—those without political rights. Slaves, of course, have no rights at all and cannot be citizens. Neither can metics (*metoikoi*), foreigners (including both non-Greeks and residents of other Greek cities) who live and work in Athens. (Metics are somewhat equivalent to the *perioikoi*, or "dwellers round about," who inhabit Sparta and a number of other Greek states.) Athenian metics are mostly merchants and tradespeople, such as potters, metalsmiths, and jewelers. Though they do not take part in government, nor own land, they do make some important contributions to the community, including providing essential goods and services, paying taxes, and serving in the army when needed.

The Athenians view full citizenship as a special and cherished right; and its loss, known as *atimia* (dishonor), is the stiffest and most dreaded penalty delivered by the courts short of exile or death. An *atimos*, a man whose citizenship had been revoked, cannot speak in the Assembly or law courts, hold public office, or enter a temple or the marketplace. And the community as a whole strictly enforces these sanctions. Any citizen who sees an *atimos* in a prohibited area is allowed to arrest him on the spot. (Such arrests are rare and the average visitor is not likely to witness one.)

The actual meetings of the Assembly of citizens take place several times a month. Of the roughly 40,000 or so male adult citizens in Attica, about 30,000 live in the countryside and only occasionally make the long trek into the city for such meetings. Attendance by at least 6,000 men is required to conduct a meeting; and if too few show up, a group of 300 specially trained slaves chases shirkers through the streets, swatting their clothes with a rope dipped in red paint (a custom that foreigners often find shocking and disquieting). Any man caught with a red stain on his tunic has to pay a fine. The meetings on the Pnyx Hill take place in the morning in the open air. A herald calls for silence. Then a priest says a prayer and sacrifices a black pig. After that, anyone who wishes to speak mounts a stone platform (the *bema*) and addresses the crowd. Visitors watching such meetings are sometimes surprised at the boisterous reactions of the crowd, which frequently boos and hisses speakers it disapproves of.

The Athenian Council

Another important democratic institution in Athens, the Council (Boule),

Most of Athens's government buildings are in the Agora. The circular structure at right-center is the Tholos, used by members of the city's Council.

works in concert with the Assembly by preparing the larger body's agenda. Council members, of which there are 500 at any given moment (raised from 400 to 500 by Cleisthenes), are chosen in the following manner. Each spring the citizens draw fifty lots (names chosen at random) from each of the city's ten tribes. Each member of a group of fifty (called a *prytany*) has to be at least thirty years old and serves on the Council for one year. (He is eligible for a second term, but not a third.) This frequent rotation of offices is designed to allow each Athenian man a seat in the Boule at least once during his lifetime.

The Council spends a good deal of the time drawing up recommendations (*probouleumata*), legislative bills dealing with state business and the community in general. The members of the Assembly then debate and vote on these bills. If a majority votes for a bill, it becomes a decree with the force of law. The Assembly can also change a bill by adding amendments, or by sending it back to the Council to be reframed. Or the voters can reject the bill outright.

In addition, the Council ensures that the decisions made by the Assembly are duly carried out by overseeing the financial and other administrative business of

Athenian Archons

As in some other Greek cities, archons (*arkhontes*) are the chief magistrates (public officials) in Athens. These include the eponymous archon, who deals with state festivals (including the famous Panathenaea and City Dionysia) and family matters; the polemarch, originally the commander in chief of the army, but now a civilian official in charge of lawsuits involving foreigners; the "king" archon, who supervises the community's religious functions; and six *thesmothetai* (keepers of the law), who oversee the law courts. Archons are chosen by lot and serve for one year. They are not eligible for reelection; however, all ex-archons automatically become members of the Areopagus, the great court that hears murder and treason cases. The visitor to Athens should note that the locals often reckon dates by the names of the eponymous archons who served in those years, although they also use the more widely accepted system of dating by the succession of the Olympiads.

the community. This task is accomplished by various Council subcommittees (boards of councillors), which closely supervise the public officials, beginning with the nine archons (chief administrators). For example, one of the Council's subcommittees inspects the state triremes[13] after construction. These men check the rigging of each ship, as well as the sheds in which the ships are stored when not in use. Such groups of councillors also inspect various public buildings. If they find any shoddy construction or misuse of public money, they report the guilty party to the Assembly, which can prosecute him in court.

Other Aspects of Democracy

Another Athenian political institution is quite familiar to those Greeks whose home cities have had occasion to oppose Athens in war. I speak of the *strategia*, the board of ten generals (*strategoi*) that the Assembly elects directly. Like the councillors, archons, and other officials, the *strategoi* serve for a year; but *unlike* the others, generals can be reelected immediately and for an unlimited number of terms. This is based on the wisdom that frequently overhauling the military leadership during a war or other national emergency can prove dangerous or even disastrous.

An Athenian general is much more than a military leader, however. The *strategoi* are often leading speakers in the Assembly. They can initiate policy both there and in the Council (which explains why many decrees have the names of generals, such as Cimon or Pericles, attached to them). Generals can also convene an Assembly meeting, and they regularly carry out the Assembly's foreign policy initiatives. When reelected frequently, a popular general is the most influential and powerful member of the community. (The most conspicuous example, of course, was Pericles, who was elected *strategos* over twenty times, fifteen of them consecutively, between 443 and 429 B.C.)

However, the Athenians have ensured that the influence of even the most popular general is limited through procedures that make public officials accountable and can even remove them from office. Before serving, each candidate has to undergo a rigorous examination (*dokimasia*), which considers his character as well as other qualifications. At any time during his term, citizens can charge him with abuse of office and bring him before the Assembly, which can fine him, remove him from office, or even condemn him to death.

In addition, the procedure of ostracism was designed to prevent one leader from amassing too much power, as well as to allow the citizens to remove a leader whose policies they feel are hindering the decision-making process. Each year the Assembly decides whether or not to hold an ostracism. If one *is* held, the citizens meet in the Agora and each scratches a name on a piece of broken pottery called an *ostrakon*. The man named is the one he believes threatens the state's political stability. If such a man receives six thousand or more of these negative votes, he has to leave the city for ten years (although he does not lose his property or citizenship).

Pericles, seen in this drawing, was both a champion of democracy and a great general.

Women's Political and Legal Status

Athenian women are citizens. But they are not *politai*, a term that means citizens but more specifically signifies "citizens with political rights." Only men in Athens are *politai*, with the rights to take part in meetings of the Assembly, hold public office, sue someone in court, sit on a jury, or serve in the military. By contrast, women are designated *astai*, meaning "citizens without political rights." An *aste* has no direct political voice but does have the civic right to take part in and/or benefit from the community's religious and economic institutions. Thus, for example, Athenian women play roles, often important ones, in various religious festivals. And though women cannot appear in court in direct ways—as jurors or litigants (prosecutors or defendants)—they *can* avail themselves of Athenian justice in indirect ways. The predominant way is for a woman's father, husband, brother, son, or other male relative to represent her interests in court. It is common, for instance, for men to prosecute or sue others in property, inheritance, adultery, and other cases directly involving women.

The Athenian Courts

Any visitor who stays in Athens for more than a few weeks quickly becomes aware that a large portion of the city's democratic apparatus is devoted to the administration of justice. Each year 6,000 men of at least thirty years of age are chosen by lot to serve as jurors, or dicasts (*dikastai*). They tend to be elderly, and thanks to legislation initiated by Pericles, they receive a daily fee. (It originally consisted of two obols, but the government raised it to three obols about forty years ago.) Paying jurors ensures that even the poorest Athenians who want to serve can do so, and also, as the comic playwright Aristophanes suggested, it constitutes a sort of old-age pension for many citizens.

The visitor who contemplates observing a local trial will find it a fascinating experience. No judge presides over such procedures; rather, a public magistrate simply makes sure that the charges are properly registered and keeps order. The litigants (the person bringing a case and the person he is accusing) gather their own evidence and witnesses and plead their own cases before the jurors. Those litigants who do not feel competent to prepare their court speeches, on which winning or losing often hinges, hire professional speechwriters (*logographai*). Demosthenes, presently the city's leading orator, long earned his living writing such speeches.

The penalties meted out are usually prescribed by law. But in some cases the prosecution can suggest one penalty and the defense another, and the jurors then decide which sentence to impose. This happened, for example, in 399 B.C. at the famous trial of Plato's old mentor, Socrates, who was accused of corrupting the youth of the community. His jury, which numbered about five hundred, voted twice, the first time to decide his guilt or innocence and the second to choose his penalty. The majority prevailed and its decision was final, for there are no appeals. (The use of such a large number of jurors, which is typ- ical of most trials, is designed to make it impractical, if not impossible, for someone to bribe or threaten enough of them to influence the verdict.)

As practically everyone knows today, Socrates was convicted and received a death sentence. Other common penalties, depending on the severity of the offense, include imprisonment, exile, partial or full loss of citizenship, confiscation

Socrates addresses his jury as he defends himself in the famous trial. When the jurists voted the second time, they decided that he should receive the death penalty.

of property, and monetary fines. Even receiving a fine is no trivial matter, for until it is paid in full, the offender and all of his descendants are barred from voting, holding public office, or sitting on juries. The visitor should also keep in mind that Athenian courts are not particularly lenient with foreigners who commit crimes while staying in the city; and some visitors have been known to remain in custody for a year or more waiting for relatives or friends to arrive and pay the fine.

CHAPTER SIX

Religious Worship and Festivals

As is true in other Greek cities, and even in barbarian (non-Greek-speaking) lands like Persia, religious belief and worship is an important cornerstone of Athenian life. Religious rituals, particularly prayer and/or sacrifice, accompany nearly every Athenian gathering, function, or important endeavor, both private and public. No pious Athenian consumes a meal, for example, without offering a portion of the food to the gods. And religious ritual attends important life-cycle events such as birth, marriage, and death. In addition, military generals perform sacrifices before battles; and major speeches delivered in the Assembly, Agora, the courts, or elsewhere often open with prayers. The Athenians also have their local religious festivals and holidays, most of which are usually unfamiliar to outsiders. However, the largest Athenian festival, the Panathenaea, is so splendid that it draws spectators from all over the Greek world.

Basics of Greek Ritual

Greek visitors to Athens need no introduction to the gods and the particulars of worship, which are essentially the same in all Greek lands. However, some basic information is provided here for the sake of Egyptians, Phoenicians, Arabs, and other foreign traders and tourists who sometimes find Greek rituals perplexing.

The gods whom the Athenians and other Greeks worship, along with the stories and traditions surrounding these deities, serve as unifying forces, reminding Greeks that beneath the surface they are all kinsmen. The major gods are known as the Olympians because early traditions claimed they dwell atop Mount Olympus, the highest mountain in Greece. (Today most Greeks view this idea as quaint and hold that the gods inhabit some faraway or invisible realm.) The ruler of these deities is Zeus, wielder of the fearsome thunderbolt. His wife is Hera, protector of marriage and children. Zeus's brother

This drawing shows the wonderful statue of Zeus designed by Phidias, the finest sculptor Athens has ever produced. It rests in the god's temple at Olympia.

Poseidon rules the seas, while Artemis is mistress of wild animals and hunting; her male twin, Apollo, is god of prophecy, music, and healing; Ares is the war god; Hephaestos is god of the forge; and Zeus's daughter Athena, with her symbols—the owl and olive tree—is goddess of wisdom and war.

It is widely believed that these and the many other gods have human form and also human emotions. Also like people, they fight among themselves and have marriages, love affairs, and children. The main factor setting the gods apart from humans is the tremendous power these divinities wield, power that can either provide for and maintain human civilization or utterly destroy it.

As holds true in most parts of the known world, the Greeks worship their gods through sacrifice and prayer, although the exact manner of these rituals differs from one place to another. Greeks usually pray standing, with the hands raised, palm upward. Unlike the Persians, the Athenians and other Greeks view kneeling in prayer (like prostrating oneself facedown before one's ruler) as unworthy of a free person. Also, prayers are usually said aloud unless the worshiper has some special reason to conceal them.

In contrast with the Egyptians, Persians, and many other non-Greeks, the Athenians and most other Greeks have no full-time priests who guide rulers and ordinary people in making important decisions. When Greek family members pray together at their home altars, the head of the household leads the ritual; while in larger public ceremonies, a clan or tribal leader or a leading state official usually takes charge. In addition, various temples and cults have staffs of caretakers and specially trained individuals who aid in sacrifices and other rituals. Any of the people described can bear the title of priest or priestess.

A few Greek priests and other individuals are trained to interpret oracles. These are messages transmitted from the gods to humans. (The sacred sites where these messages are given and also the priestesses who deliver them are also called oracles.) No oracles exist in Attica. So on those occasions when the state feels it necessary to ask for divine guidance, the Athenians send messengers to one or both of the two most famous oracular shrines. One is at Apollo's sanctuary at Delphi (in central Greece), the other at Zeus's sanctuary at Dodona (in northwestern Greece).

Athena and Athens

While all Greeks hold these gods and their general worship in common, individual cities have their local favorites. Each has a patron deity who is thought to watch over and protect its inhabitants and with whom it strongly identifies itself. As people everywhere know well, one way to ensure that a city's divine patron remains close to the community, the better to watch over and protect the inhabitants, is to provide that deity with its own house or shelter. Accordingly, the Athenians have erected several temples dedicated to their patron deity, Athena, the most famous and splendid of which is the Parthenon on the Acropolis. (Athens also has temples and shrines dedicated to Zeus, Artemis, Hephaestos, and other gods.) Inside the building's main room

(*cella*) stands the goddess's cult image (statue), a magnificent creation almost forty feet high and covered with sheets of beaten gold.

Most people think that from time to time Athena actually comes to rest within this and her other temples; so these structures are seen as sacred places. Naturally enough, so are the surrounding grounds, which typically feature outdoor sacrificial altars and areas for individual or group prayer. (To respect the god's privacy, of

The Athenian Calendar

Each Greek city-state has its own calendar, with its own local names of the months, which are most often named after religious festivals. Because many visitors to Athens are not familiar with the Athenian (Attic) months, they are listed below.

Hekatombaion (July)
Metageitnion (August)
Boedromion (September)
Pyanopsion (October)
Maimakterion (November)
Poseideon (December)
Gamelion (January)
Anthesterion (February)
Elaphebolion (March)
Mounichion (April)
Thargelion (May)
Skirophorion (June)

An oracle swoons before answering a question posed by a religious pilgrim at Apollo's sacred temple at Delphi. The Delphic oracle is the most renowned in all Greece.

course, no worship takes place inside the building, as it does in some foreign lands.)

Athena's cult image in the Parthenon, known as the Athena Parthenos, is only one of several manifestations of the goddess. She is seen as having a number of different sides to her character, each of which personifies a special talent or physical or mental attribute. In Greek homes a room where a young woman, ideally a virgin, dwells before her marriage is often referred to as a parthenon. Athena Parthenos means "Athena the Virgin," an image emphasizing her feminine beauty and the purity of her wisdom. By contrast, Athena Promachos (Athena the Warrior Champion) and Athena Nike (Athena the Victor) are images stressing her physical strength, courage, and fearsome fighting skills. Other manifestations of Athena include Hygieia (Goddess of Health) and Ergane (the Worker).

The relationship between Athena and Athens is a very old and venerable one. And the Athenians have collected a rich collection of popular stories about the goddess, which the visitor is likely to hear frequently repeated in barber shops, gymnasia, schools, and elsewhere, especially on festival days. One of the most famous is the one in which Athena and Poseidon engaged in a contest to decide which of them would become Athens's patron. (For more about this incident, see the chapter on Athens's history.) Another tradition popular among

Athena Promachos (the Warrior Champion) poses with her mighty spear and shield in this vase painting. As Athens's patron, the goddess protects the city.

Athenians holds that Athena sent an olive-wood statue of herself hurtling out of the sky. The spot on which it landed, near the Acropolis's northern edge, became the site for the Erechtheum, the temple that houses her sacred statue, the Athena Polias (Athena of the City).

The Greater Panathenaea

Of course, Athena and her wooden statue play a central role in Athens's most important and renowned religious festival—the Panathenaea. (For the sake of non-Greeks, the name translates variously as "All the Athenians," or "Rites of All Athenians.") The festival's religious cere-

monies, feasts, and musical and athletic contests attract visitors from Greek lands far and wide. It is held annually, but the Athenians celebrate it with special pomp every fourth year, when it is called the Greater Panathenaea. Travelers should be aware that during the festival's seven or eight days (between the twenty-third and thirtieth days of the Athenian month of Hekatombaion, or July), the city becomes extremely crowded, and lodgings are practically impossible to find.

The highlight of the festival usually takes place on the twenty-eighth day of the month. Following the time-honored route known as the Panathenaic Way, a

The Panathenaic Procession stops near the Parthenon and Erechtheum on the summit of the Acropolis. The festival is held with extra pomp every fourth year.

huge and stately procession begins at the Thriasian Gate in the city's northwest wall. The marchers come from all social classes and groups. Besides archons, council members, generals, and soldiers, they include a number of elderly men chosen for their handsome looks; called the *thallophoroi*, they wear elegant robes and carry olive branches. Following them come children bearing trays, water jars, and baskets holding utensils that will later be used in the sacrifices. Visitors should take special note of the *kanephoroi*, young virgin girls selected from the city's noblest families; these young women also carry objects for the sacrifices. Among the other marchers are selected metics, who by tradition carry bronze or silver trays filled with cakes and honeycombs; ex-slaves, who bear oak branches; and slaves, who lead the animals that are to be sacrificed later.

Athena's Sacred Robe

The procession makes it way through the Agora, as thousands watch spellbound along the roadway. Finally, it reaches the base of the Acropolis; and after ascending the steps and reaching the summit, the marchers congregate in the open space between the Parthenon and Erechtheum. Here, the central ceremony transpires, involving the festival's principal single element—the *peplos*, Athena Polias's sacred robe. The *peplos* is conveyed in the grand procession as a sail attached to the mast of a miniature ship carried on a wagon (to emphasize Athens's naval supremacy). When the marchers reach the base of

History of the Panathenaea

Athens's chief religious festival—the Panathenaea—is very ancient, having originated sometime in the Age of Heroes. Two different myths are associated with its establishment, the first of which claims that an early king named Erechtheus started the festival to honor Athena's victory over one of the giants who fought against the Olympian gods. In the other story, the Athenian hero Theseus completely reorganized the festival after he unified the towns of Attica into a political whole, creating the Athenian state. The Panathenaea underwent another major reorganization in 566 B.C., and after that it was the city's greatest festival.

the Acropolis, some citizens remove the robe from the cart; then two prechosen Athenians, a man and a boy, step forward and fold it with great care as everyone watches in hushed silence.[14]

Once the marchers reach the temples atop the hill, the man and boy present the *peplos* to Athena's high priestess. The garment is destined to be draped around the goddess's wooden statue in the Erechtheum, replacing the one from previous festival. (Several months before

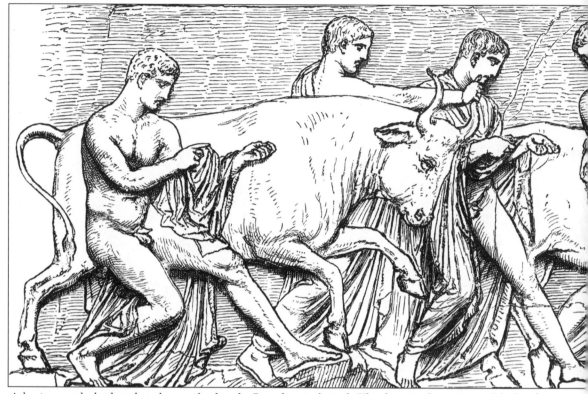

Athenian youths lead cattle to be sacrificed in the Panathenaic festival. This drawing depicts part of the band of sculptures in the frieze on the Parthenon's south side.

a Panathenaea, the high priestess begins the creation of a new robe by setting the yarn in the loom. She is assisted by four girls between the ages of seven and eleven, the *arrephoroi*, who live on the Acropolis for a year while in special service to the goddess; two or more other maidens, the *ergastinai*, then proceed to weave the robe. Following the Panathenaea, a group of women from the Attic clan Praxiergidai take charge of the robe; and later, in a ceremony called the Plynteria, which takes place on the twenty-fifth of Mounichion, or April, they wash and dress the statue.)

After the sacred robe has been presented to the goddess, a large number of animal sacrifices take place at Athena's great altar, located near the eastern ends of the Parthenon and Erechtheum. In each Panathenaea, a hundred Athenian cows and many sheep and other animals brought by visitors from other city-states are sacrificed. Following Greek tradition, the worshipers drape flower garlands over the animals and lead them to the altar. After purifying the altar with water, a priest purifies the animals by sprinkling barley grains on them. Then he stuns each with a club and cuts its throat.

Finally, he and his assistants slaughter the animal; wrap the bones and organs in fat and burn them, so that the smoke will rise up and nourish and appease the goddess; and divide the meat among the worshipers. They cook the meat and enjoy a feast, which visitors are allowed to join.

The Anthesteria

Such large-scale public sacrifices are routine at the many other religious festivals and observances celebrated in Attica. Visitors are welcome to observe a number of these celebrations, the more important of which are described below. The Anthesteria, held from the eleventh to thirteenth of the month Anthesterion (February), is a perennial favorite. Because Dionysus, whom it honors, is a fertility god, it appropriately takes place in the season when the first flower blossoms and other signs of coming spring begin to appear. The first day of the festival, the so-called Jar-Opening, witnesses worshipers tasting samples of new wine and sacrificing them by pouring them over the altar.

On the second day of the Anthesteria, called Wine-Jugs, the worshipers march in a procession in which a painted image (or sometimes a masked actor) of Dionysus rides in a cart. Also on that day, it is customary for everyone, including small children, to drink wine. In addition, the children receive gifts, including miniature wine jugs and toys.

Visitors to Athens take heed that the festival's third day, Pots, is more somber and ominous. Pots containing boiled vegetables are sacrificed to satisfy and ward off the spirits of the dead, which, many Athenians believe, roam about at will. At the end of the day (and the festival), people customarily shout, "Go away, you dreaded spirits! The Anthesteria is over!" or words to that effect. The hope is that these words, invoked in Dionysus's name, will keep the ghosts away for several months to come.

Demeter's Mysteries

Highlighting Boedromion (September) is the renowned festival of the Eleusinian Mysteries, dedicated to Demeter. (Foreign visitors often identify her with their own goddesses who bring fertility or oversee agriculture. Many Egyptians equate her with their Isis, for example; and the Romans, who inhabit a large city-state in Italy, call her Ceres.) The focus of Demeter's celebration is the cult of the Mysteries, which requires an initiation to join. Membership is open to all, male or female, free or slave.

New initiates first purify themselves by bathing in the sea, then sacrifice a young pig and join the other members in a great procession almost as large as the one that opens the Greater Panathenaea. The parade begins at the Eleusinion, a small temple located near the foot of the Acropolis. There, the cult's "sacred objects" are stored. The marchers veil these objects and solemnly carry them to Demeter's sanctuary at Eleusis, about twelve miles west of Athens's urban center. The festival's climax takes place in the sanctuary's initiation hall (the Telesterion), where a priest or priestess reveals the sacred objects to the initiates.

(Important note: It is vital that foreigners be cautious about discussing the nature of these objects, as well as the initiations, all of which are secret, hence the name "Mysteries." The members closely guard their secrecy and have been known to react violently to those who threaten to compromise it. A few generations ago, the great tragic playwright Aeschylus learned this the hard way. Quite by accident it seems, a line in one of his works described part of the secret ceremony, and several dozen of Demeter's followers, who happened to be in the audience, rushed the stage intending to lynch him. His suc-

cessful claim of sanctuary at the theater's altar stone was the only thing that saved the terrified man.)

Other Athenian Festivals

Another prominent Attic festival that honors Demeter—the Thesmophoria (held for three days, the eleventh to thirteenth of Pyanopsion, or October)—is celebrated all over Greece, so the description provided here for the sake of non-Greeks will be brief. Only women take part in this festival, which consists of fertility rituals designed to ensure a plentiful harvest of cereal crops. On the first day, the women camp out on a hillside; on the second, they fast; and on the third, they conduct various rituals involving plants and animals. Much concerning this festival is kept secret among the women who take part. And non-Greeks, especially men, will be wise to steer clear of the areas of worship on these days.

On the fourteenth day of Skirophorion (June), the Athenians hold the Bouphonia (also called the Dipolieia). Outsiders may well find this brief festival, dedicated to Zeus Polias (Zeus of the City), somewhat strange. As worshipers watch, a priest places several handfuls of barley and wheat on an altar, after which some men coax a bull to approach the altar. Just as the bull begins eating the grain, the priest leaps forward and kills it with a poleax (a small ax used for slaughtering cattle). Then he drops the ax and runs away. Finally, the worshipers try the ax (not the priest!) for murder, invariably find the weapon guilty,

A bull is led toward a sacrificial altar in this beautiful vase painting.

and throw it into the sea. (Athenians give various explanations for this odd ritual, the origins of which are very ancient and obscure. The most common version is that, having eaten from the god's sacred altar, the bull itself has become sacred; so killing it constitutes murder. Someone or something has to be punished for the offense, and better it be the ax than the priest, who is always careful not to touch the beast lest he share in the guilt.)

Some of the other Athenian festivals of note include the Theogamia, held on the twenty-seventh day of Gamelion (January), which celebrates the sacred marriage between the gods Zeus and Hera; and the City Dionysia, held in Elaphebolion (March), widely famous for its dramatic contests. (For details of the City Dionysia and its theatrical events, see the chapter on sightseeing in Athens.) Numerous smaller celebrations and individual sacrifices are observed throughout the year. (In addition to these religious festivals, there are several secular ones that feature sacrifices. One is the Synoecia, which celebrates Theseus's ancient union of the peoples of Attica. Others include the Democratia, observing Athens's democratic institutions, and various local celebrations held by Attic tribes, clans, and villages.)

CHAPTER SEVEN

Athletics and Recreation

The visitor will find the Athenians just as avid in their interest for athletic games as other Greeks. And Athens offers a considerable range of athletic activities that visitors can both watch and participate in. Non-Greeks sometimes express surprise and confusion at the wide variety of Greek games and the heavy emphasis the Greeks place on both physical conditioning and athletic competition. Indeed, the word Greeks use to describe such competition—*agon*—means a struggle; and they employ the same word for other serious kinds of contests, including battles and lawsuits.

It is hardly a secret that the Athenians glorify athletic prowess and the ideal physical form required to excel in athletics; after all, statues of muscular naked athletes adorn every corner of the city. This fascination for physical form and achievement runs deeper, though. A majority of male Athenians adhere to the concept of *kalokagathia*, roughly translating as the

"mental (or moral) and physical ideal." It stresses striving for a combination of physical and intellectual (or moral) excellence in order to develop a rounded and complete personality. Before Athens became a democratic state, it was fashionable only among aristocrats, since they were the only ones with the leisure time and money needed for training and competing. But the rise of democracy, with its ideals of social equality and the spread of state-sponsored education for all male citizens, eventually popularized the concept of *kalokagathia*; and today a good many Athenians glorify a keen mind in a strong, athletic body.

The degree to which this notion has become ingrained in the popular consciousness can be seen in the city's social customs and institutions. Gymnasia, in which patrons receive both physical and academic training, are an integral feature of the city's life. And the athletic games held at the Panathenaea are eagerly anticipated and renowned throughout all of Greece.

Big Rewards for Winning Athletes

At the same time, a number of Athenian men train hard for the larger Panhellenic (all-Greek) games, the most renowned of all being the Olympics, of course. Every four years these men eagerly await the arrival of the Truce-Bearers. (Non-Greeks take note: These are three heralds from Elis, the city that hosts the Olympics. They travel to every Greek city to announce the exact date of the coming games, which varies from one Olympiad to the next, and invite all to attend. They also announce the sacred Olympic truce, or *ekecheiria*. For its duration of three months, all participating states are forbidden from making war or imposing death penalties, thus ensuring safe passage for the thousands of competitors, spectators, and religious pilgrims who attend the games.)

Athenians make their way toward Olympia to witness the Olympic Games, held in honor of Zeus. Once there, most spectators camp out under the stars.

The athletes who take part in these large-scale contests have good reason to train hard. They know that if they win, Athens will heap honors and prizes on them and worship them almost like gods for the rest of their lives. Indeed, to encourage Athenian athletes to win such events and thereby bring the city honor and glory, the government offers monetary rewards for winners at the Olympics and

The victor of an Olympic chariot race receives a hero's welcome when he returns home to Athens.

other Panhellenic games (including the contests at the Greater Panathenaea). An Athenian Olympic victor receives five hundred drachmas, for example; and a winner at the Isthmian Games gets a hundred drachmas. (To appreciate the enormity of these prizes, the visitor should keep in mind that an average Athenian worker makes about two drachmas per day.)

Winners also receive valuable bronze tripods, ornamental cups, and jars of olive oil, which they can sell for a profit. A winning runner at the Panathenaic Games, for instance, receives one hundred jars of olive oil, valued at around twelve hundred drachmas. This means that an athlete can earn the equivalent of about four years' salary by winning a single footrace! With his twelve hundred drachmas, he can purchase six or seven medium-priced slaves, or a flock of a hundred sheep, or two or three houses in Athens's urban center.

In addition, Athens awards its winning athletes free meals for life (a practice called *sitesis*). The visitor can read for himself the inscription carved on a stone outside the Council building in the Agora: "All those who have won the athletic event at the Olympic, Pythian, Isthmian, or Nemean games shall have the right to eat free of charge in the city hall and also have other honors in addition to the free meals."[15]

Panathenaic Events: Footraces

A few other Greek cities reward their winning athletes with prizes and free meals in

The Panathenaic Runners

Hundreds of runners compete in the running events at the Panathenaea. Because it would be too chaotic for them all to race at once, there are several preliminary heats for each event. The runners draw lots from a bronze bowl to determine who will run in each heat; and the winners of the heats face one another in the final showdown. Following custom, the runners approach the starting line and do some last-minute warm-up exercises, including running in place, deep knee-bends, and practice starts. When everyone is ready, the chief judge signals for the start with a shout of "Go!" ("*Apite!*") False starts occur only rarely, perhaps because the judges punish the offenders by having them publicly flogged. Once the runners leave the starting gate, they dash to the turning post (*kampter*) at the opposite end of the stadium; in races longer than the stade, they make a hairpin turn around the post and then run the opposite way.

a like manner. So if the visitor has come to compete in Athens's Panathenaic Games (which are open to non-Athenians as well as Athenians), he may be fortunate enough to experience such honors himself. The much more numerous visitors who come merely to watch the games will have to content themselves with the thrill of witnessing some of the finest contests in all of Greece. The Athenians added these games to the Panathenaea when they reorganized the festival in 566 B.C. Since that time, they have become the most prestigious local games held by any Greek state, only slightly lower in stature than the Olympics. In Attica itself, the Panathenaic Games, which honor Athena, have come to overshadow the local tribal competitions, which still take place each year.

The Panathenaic contests, held in the Agora, fall into two broad categories,

the first being the familiar events also held in the Olympics and most other Panhellenic games. As at Olympia, for instance, footraces are among the most prestigious events in the Athenian games. The staples are the stade, a sprint of about six hundred feet; the *diaulos*, a two-stade run; and the *dolichos*, a longer run of twenty-four stades. The racecourse is wide enough to accommodate only about ten runners at a time; so initial heats are held for each race, with the winners of the heats competing in the final contest for the prizes. There is also a stade for boys (under eighteen).

Another important Panathenaic footrace is the race in armor, the *hoplitodromos* (which takes its name from "hoplite," the term describing a heavily armored infantry soldier). Each runner wears a bronze helmet and greaves [16] and

Contestants taking part in the grueling race in armor dash toward the finish line during one of the most exciting moments in the Panathenaic athletic competitions.

carries a bronze shield (*hoplon*). The race is two stades in length (and therefore equivalent to the *diaulos*). The *hoplitodromos,* with its armored men clanking along—occasionally bumping into and falling over one another—can sometimes appear humorous. A number of Athenian playwrights, including Aristophanes, who prospered in the last century, have poked fun at racing hoplites.

Panathenaic Events: Combat, Pentathlon, and Equestrian

Just as popular as the footraces at the Panathenaea are the combat, or "heavy," events. These include wrestling, boxing, and the pankration. (Non-Greeks should take note that the pankration is a very strenuous combination of boxing and wrestling in which punching, kicking, throwing, pressure locks, and strangling are all allowed. Only biting and eye gouging are forbidden. A match ends only when one fighter surrenders, loses consciousness, or dies.)

The pentathlon, a grueling test of overall athletic prowess, is also quite popular. It consists of five events—the stade, wrestling, the javelin throw, discus throw, and running broad jump. The wrestling matches are usually the last of the five to be staged.

The Panathenaea also features equestrian (horse) races. The participants are most often well-to-do, mainly because breeding and racing horses requires generous amounts of both land and money. The events include a race for solo horses ridden by jockeys and contests for two- and four-horse chariots. The owner of the horse or horses, who may or may not be the driver or rider, claims the victory and garners the prizes.

As visitors who have attended the Panathenaea before can attest, the equestrian events often provide heart-stopping excitement. This is partly because of the very real dangers involved. Indeed, crashes and spills in the frantic eight-mile-long, four-horse chariot contest (the *tethrippon*) are almost routine. The great Athenian playwright Sophocles did an admirable job of describing a typical series of racetrack collisions in *Electra:*

One wrestler applies a body lock while his opponent attempts to break the hold by tripping him. Meanwhile, a judge looks on, his rod ready to punish a rule-breaker.

To begin with, all went well with every chariot. Then the Athenian's tough colts took the bit in their teeth and on the turn from the sixth to the seventh lap, ran head-on into the African. The accident led to other upsets and collisions, till the field . . . was a sea of wrecked and capsized chariots. The Athenian driver had seen what was coming and was clever enough to draw aside and bide his time while the oncoming wave crashed into inextricable confusion. Orestes was driving past, purposely holding his team back and pinning his faith to the final spurt; and now, seeing only one rival left in, with an exultant shout to his swift horses he drove hard ahead and the two teams raced neck and neck, now one now the other gaining a lead. . . . But at the last [lap], Orestes misjudged the turn, slackened his left rein before the horse was safely round the bend, and so fouled the [turning] post. The hub was smashed across, and he was hurled over the rail entangled in the severed reins, and as he fell his horses ran wild across the course.[17]

Visitors to Athens usually notice that one equestrian event held in the Panathenaic Games is not on the Olympic program. This is the *apobates*, or chariot-dismounting race. It features hoplites, either in full armor or nude with helmet and shield, riding chariots. These athletes (called *apobatai*, or "dismounters") jump off their chariots partway through the race and run the rest of the way on foot.

Athens's Tribal Contests

The second category of Panathenaic contests includes events that are open only to Athenian citizens. Among these are some military-style equestrian events not held

The Women's Games

Non-Greeks who attend the Olympic Games at Elis every four years are quick to notice that women are not allowed to compete in or watch the events. However, so that women will not feel totally excluded from the sporting scene, the people of Elis hold a small separate women's festival and games at Olympia every four years. It is called the Heraea because it honors the goddess Hera. Sixteen Elean women organize and run the games, which feature one event, a footrace of about five hundred feet, with separate heats for different age groups. The women run with their hair down, their tunics pulled up above their knees, and their right breasts and shoulders bared. The winners receive crowns made of olive branches and a share of the ox slaughtered in Hera's honor at the festival.

A driver carefully maneuvers his chariot in front of an opponent who is threatening to overtake him in one of the exciting races held at the Panathenaea.

in the Olympics. In one, a "procession" for two-horse chariots, the teams are judged on their abilities at precision marching and drilling. Another event features a rider on a moving horse who throws a javelin at a target.

Outside of the Panathenaea, Athenians-only events predominate in the tribal contests. These are larger and more prestigious versions of competitions that were originally held locally by single tribes and/or their respective clans. One very popular event is the "Pyrrhic dance," which tradition holds was first performed by Athena directly after her birth from Zeus's head. A tribal team of several men,

carrying spears and shields (and often nude), go through a complex and vigorous series of precision moves in unison. Plato described it this way:

> The warrior dance . . . rightly termed Pyrrhic [fiery] . . . imitates the modes of avoiding blows and missiles by dropping or giving way, or springing aside, or rising up or falling down; also . . . the imitation of archery and the hurling of javelins, and all sorts of blows. [18]

Among the other tribal events are various torch races, both team and individual. One team event is a relay race in which members of a tribal contingent of forty runners pass a lit torch to one another, each running a leg of about two hundred feet (the total distance covered being just over a mile and a half). There is also a solo torch race in which the contestants run into the city from an altar set up in the countryside to honor Prometheus (which is appropriate, considering that he was the god whom legend claims gave fire to the human race).

Gymnasia and Assorted Sports Activities

Seeing the tremendous popularity of the Panathenaic and tribal athletic contests, the visitor will hardly be surprised at the enthusiasm Athenians of all social classes display for physical training. Facilities for training and exercise, including the gymnasia, are prominent features in Athenian life. (Note to non-Greeks: The word "gymnasium" comes from *gymnos*,

Young athletes train at an Athenian gymnasium. The two fellows grappling at lower left are in the final stages of a boxing contest.

meaning "naked," since Greek athletes often train and compete in the nude.) An average gymnasium consists of a building with rooms for changing, bathing, and socializing; an adjacent field for practicing various sports; and, in keeping with the physical-mental ideal, some small libraries, reading rooms, and/or lecture halls dedicated to higher learning.

Perhaps the most famous local gymnasium is the Academy, founded by Plato in 385 B.C., which since his recent death has become a popular tourist stop. It is located beyond the city walls about three-quarters of a mile northwest of the Thriasian Gate. It is right on the main road, so the traveler cannot miss it. Plato hoped that the young men who studied with him there would gain the philosophical and ethical insights that would make them good statesmen. Whether or not this dream will be realized remains to be seen.

Athens also has a number of *palaestrae*, or "wrestling schools," although these facilities are used for general exercise and academic instruction as well as for wrestling. Regarding the latter, its popularity among Athenian males cannot be overstated. In fact, wrestling training constitutes the most important part of physical education for Athenian boys. Boys and young men often wrestle informally; and most accomplished Athenian adult males enjoy and participate in wrestling as much as they do reading or discussing politics with friends.

The visitor who desires to stay in shape while in Athens will find other sports activities besides wrestling open to him. These include the team ball game *episkyros*,[19] boating, and swimming. Hunting is also popular, especially among members of the upper classes, who can best afford horses and packs of hunting hounds. Common game in the area include wild boar, bears, fox, deer, rabbits, and birds. For sheer physical conditioning, however, nothing can match wrestling.

CHAPTER EIGHT

Sightseeing in Athens

Athens's urban center boasts enough attractions to keep a visitor busy for several days. They range from political institutions and gatherings, to monumental stone temples, to theatrical performances, to world-renowned paintings, not to mention the Agora itself, one of the largest shopping districts in the Greek world. Below, the traveler will find directions to and descriptions of the most famous sights; for the sake of convenience, the location of each sight is reckoned using the Acropolis as a starting point, since it is visible from all points in the city.

The Acropolis Complex

Athens's chief tourist attraction remains the complex of religious structures atop

The Athenian Acropolis is the most famous of all the acropoli in Greece. This model shows the Propylaea and temple complex from the northwest.

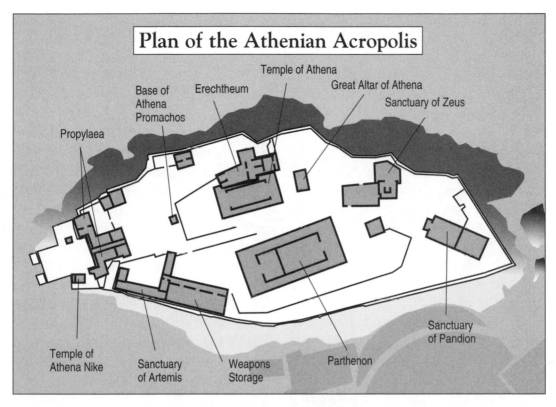

Plan of the Athenian Acropolis

Base of Athena Promachos

Erechtheum

Temple of Athena

Great Altar of Athena

Sanctuary of Zeus

Propylaea

Sanctuary of Pandion

Temple of Athena Nike

Sanctuary of Artemis

Weapons Storage

Parthenon

the city's central hill. The complex can be seen for miles in every direction; and sailors far out at sea say that they can sometimes see sunlight reflecting off the shield and spear of the Athena Promachos (the huge bronze statue created by the master sculptor Phidias in the last century). Most of the existing structures on the hill were erected in Phidias's day to replace those destroyed by the Persians when they occupied the city during the invasion of King Xerxes in 480 B.C. Pericles, Athens's leading statesman in that era, instigated and supervised much of the work, except for those parts that were finished after his untimely death (of plague in 429 B.C.). The Acropolis complex, highlighted by

the magnificent Parthenon, never fails to impress and move those who see it.

The visitor wishing to climb to the complex must approach the Acropolis from the southwest, where he will find a wide set of marble stairs winding up the hill's western flank. As he ascends, he will first encounter the small Temple of Athena Nike, perched on a stone bastion rising from the right side of the stairway. Like the other temples on the hill, it is dedicated to Athena. Just beyond the temple is the Propylaea, the massive gateway to the summit. The gateway consists of a central hall covered by a roof supported by a huge colonnade. Rectangular colonnaded wings project left (north) and right (south) from the central hall. The south wing rests just behind the Temple of Athena Nike; and the Propylaea's north wing contains a gallery of paintings that are worth stopping in to see. Among them are one that shows the hero Odysseus taking Philoctetes' bow on the isle of Lemnos,[20] and another that depicts Orestes slaying Aegisthus.[21]

Though quite splendid in and of itself, the Propylaea provides but a foretaste of the wonders to come. Once through the gateway, the visitor finds himself on the hill's roughly flat summit. Immediately ahead looms the lofty Athena Promachos, which, many people say, appears to be guarding the complex, a mighty presence that is simultaneously intimidating and reassuring. Immediately to the right of the gateway is the small sanctuary (*temenos*) of the goddess Artemis. It consists of a spacious open court backed by a colonnaded hall that runs for about 140 feet along the southern wall of the Acropolis. Just beyond the sanctuary, and of roughly equal length, looms the Chalcotheca (the storage shed for the weapons that stand ready in case the hill comes under attack). Visitors should note that the latter is guarded day and night and open only to certain government officials.

Turning one's back on the Chalcotheca and walking north, one passes through a small portico (columned porch) and emerges about fifty feet from the right (south) side of the Athena Promachos. A stone retaining wall rises behind the statue, sectioning off the wide terrace that holds the sanctuary of the Erechtheum. If one walks around the northern section of the wall, he will reach

The eastern façade of the Erechtheum has a lovely colonnade featuring six Ionic columns. The famous Porch of the Maidens can be seen in the distance at left.

The Parthenon—dedicated to Athena—is widely seen as the most beautiful temple in Greece.

the western porch of this lovely temple. It features four porches in all (north, south, east, and west), laid out in a unique split-level arrangement. The south-facing porch, which is perhaps the most famous, is often called the Porch of the Maidens because the six columns holding up its roof are in the form of maidens in flowing robes. These are the Karyatids.[22]

Inside the Erechtheum rests the sacred olive-wood statue of Athena that legend claims came hurtling out of the sky and landed where the temple now sits. Actually the structure is the latest in a succession of temples that have housed the statue on this spot. All have borne the name Erechtheum, derived from Erechtheus, one of the city's early kings. Today he is often viewed as a sort of partner to Athena or custodian of her temples, and painters and sculptors often picture him as a serpent guarding the goddess.

Situated about 50 feet southeast of the Erechtheum is the great altar of Athena, where the sacrifices take place during the Panathenaea. And about 90 feet farther to the east lies the sanctuary of Zeus. Numerous smaller altars, as well as hun-

dreds of elegant bronze and marble statues, line the marble walkways and terraces within the sanctuaries, giving the whole place a look of crowded splendor.

A Building that Transcends Time

All of these marvelous buildings, porticoes, shrines, and statues pale, however, in comparison with the structure that dominates the entire summit—the Parthenon. Rising from the hill's south-central area, it is a breathtaking sight from every direction and angle. The great architect Ictinus designed it, Phidias created its sculptures, and it was completed in 432 B.C., shortly before the outbreak of the Peloponnesian War. But all who see this incredible building agree that it transcends any particular time; that it appears impressive in old age and at the same time newly built, truly a structure for the ages.

The dimensions of the Parthenon are as follows. It is 228 feet long, 101 feet wide, and 65 feet high. It is an octa-style temple (having eight columns across the front and back and seventeen down the sides, counting the corner columns twice). This alone

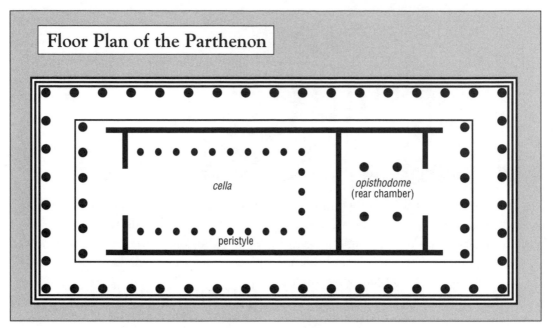

Floor Plan of the Parthenon

cella

opisthodome
(rear chamber)

peristyle

sets it on a grander scale than most Greek temples, which are almost all hexa-style (six by thirteen columns, counting the corner columns twice).

The visitor is urged to walk around the whole perimeter of the building slowly so as not to miss any of the sculptures, no two of which are the same. The cluster of twenty-two larger-than-life-size statues in the front (western) pediment (the triangular space beneath the slanted roof) depicts a scene familiar to all Athenians—the contest between Athena and Poseidon for possession of Attica.

Below the pediment are fourteen of the structure's ninety-two metopes (rectangular panels bearing relief sculptures), which together make up the Doric frieze. The overall theme of all the scenes depicted on the metopes is Greece's, and especially Athens's, triumph over the forces of

barbarism and disorder. The west-facing metopes show the Athenians fighting the Amazons (a battle known as the Amazonomachy). During the Age of Heroes, the story goes, these legendary warrior-women landed at Marathon, like the Persians did later; also like the Persians, the Amazons attacked Athens, only to be driven off.

If one turns right and walks along the temple's south-facing side, he will see thirty-two metopes that show warfare between the Lapiths and Centaurs (the Centauromachy). In this myth the Lapiths, members of an early Greek tribe, defeated the half-human, half-horse Centaurs, who had tried to carry off the Lapith women. Reaching the Parthenon's east end, one finds fourteen metopes depicting episodes from the primeval war between the giants and Olympian gods (the Gigantomachy). Above them, in the eastern pediment, are the huge figures portraying Athena's dramatic birth from her father's head, witnessed by a bevy of astonished deities. Continuing on to the north side, one finds the remaining metopes, this time showing famous scenes from the Trojan War, an earlier victory of West over East, not unlike Athens's defeat of the Persians at Marathon.

The Parthenon's Ionic Frieze

In addition to its Doric frieze, made up of the scenes on the ninety-two metopes, the Parthenon has an Ionic frieze. The latter is located high up along the inside of the main colonnade, so it is usually in shadow and a bit hard to see; but it is well worth the effort. Its sculptures, designed by Phidias, form a continuous panel that stretches around the whole building and depicts the parade of humans, horses, and chariots during Athens's grandest festival—the Panathenaea. On the building's western flank are horsemen, some riding abreast, others by themselves. This theme carries forward onto the north side, where the horsemen occupy almost half of that portion of the frieze. In front of the riders are chariots, followed by groups of walking figures, among them elders, pitcher-carriers, tray-bearers, musicians, and slaves leading cattle and sheep for the sacrifices. On the east side, young girls carry various vessels and some men lean on walking sticks while they converse. In front of them are several gods, who appear larger than the mortal figures. The southern part of the frieze is similar in scope to the northern one.

This horseman appears in the north-facing section of the great Ionic frieze.

77

The Athena Parthenos

The visitor must not miss the Parthenon's interior, which is as impressive and beautiful as its exterior. The *cella* (main room) measures 108 feet by 62 feet, and the ceiling is 43 feet high. A double colonnade (one row of columns standing atop another) divides the room into a U-shaped central area, flanked by narrow aisles. Standing inside this central area and completely dominating the *cella*'s interior is the Athena Parthenos, the stunning thirty-eight-foot-high statue designed by Phidias.

The goddess Athena is known to assume many guises and moods. Here she is in thoughtful repose, a contrast with her bold, stalwart statue inside the Parthenon.

It is made of ivory and beaten gold. The statue stands upright and sports a tunic that reaches to the feet. The image of a sphinx (monster with a woman's face) adorns the middle of the goddess's helmet, while the helmet's sides bear griffins (beasts with the bodies of lions and the wings of eagles). On her majestic breastplate can be seen an ivory face of Medusa (a female monster with snakes for hair). In one hand, Athena holds a six-foot-tall figure of the goddess Victory; in the other, she holds a spear. Meanwhile, at her feet rests her shield. And near the shield is a serpent, which represents her attendant, Erechtheus.

One is advised to pay special attention to the battle scenes Phidias carved onto the surfaces of the huge shield. On the outside, part of the Amazonomachy is visible, while a portion of the Gigantomachy appears on the inside. An interesting controversy surrounded the outer scene shortly after the statue was completed. Two of the figures fighting the Amazons are said to have looked exactly like Phidias and his friend Pericles, and several angry Athenians berated the sculptor for what they considered both sacrilege and undue vanity.

In summary, the Acropolis complex is a joy to behold and promises to make Athens the focal point of avid tourism for a long time to come. Pericles himself recognized the special, timeless qualities of the place. "Future ages will wonder at us," he confidently predicted, "as the present age wonders at us now."[23] Only time will tell if this bold prophecy will be fulfilled.

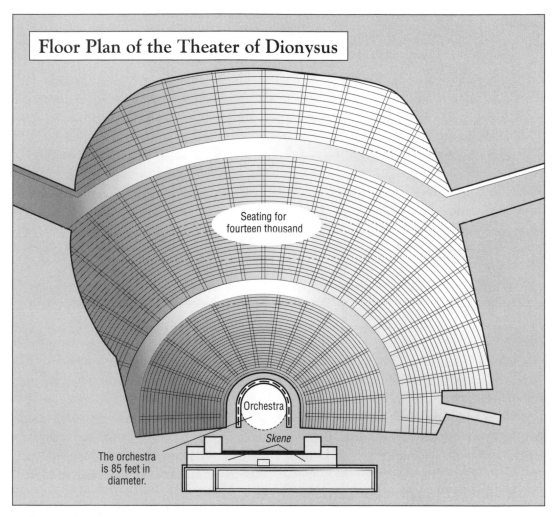

Floor Plan of the Theater of Dionysus

Seating for fourteen thousand

Orchestra

Skene

The orchestra is 85 feet in diameter.

The Theater of Dionysus

Prophecies aside, the visitor is certain to be fulfilled by attending the theater. Today a large number of Greek cities have theaters. But this unique combination of art form and public entertainment originated in Athens less than two centuries ago. A series of informal songs and speeches recited by worshipers in roadside religious processions evolved into formal dramatic competitions held in large pub-lic facilities. These contests became part of the City Dionysia, the religious festival held in March in honor of the fertility god Dionysus. (Such competitions are also presented on a smaller scale at the Rural Dionysia, held in December, and the Lenaea, also dedicated to Dionysus, held in January.)

The first Athenian theater was erect-ed perhaps in the early 530s B.C. It was in the Agora and consisted of a circular

Local Theatrical Backers

Foreign visitors to the Theater of Dionysus are often amazed at the lavish production values of the plays, which feature elaborate masks, costumes, large numbers of actors, and so forth; and the question most commonly asked is where the money for these spectacles comes from. The answer is that it derives from a system of public contributions called liturgies (*leitourgiai*, or "the people's burdens"). The Athenian government requires well-to-do citizens to pay for public services that benefit the whole community. These include theatrical productions, the erection of statues and monuments, distribution of food at religious festivals, and so on. Each year the names of new such arts patrons are chosen, in rotation, from lists of better-off citizens. The backer of a play is called a *choregus*. He can expect to spend an average of 500 to 2,500 drachmas to mount a single play; although some *choregoi* spend 4,000, 5,000, or even more. Most take pride in this duty, partly because it brings them considerable prestige.

"dancing place," or orchestra, where the actors performed; a central altar (*thymele*), for sacrificing to Dionysus; and an audience area (*theatron*) with wooden bleachers. In 499 B.C. these bleachers collapsed in the middle of a performance, killing many of the spectators.

Following this unfortunate incident, the Athenians constructed the Theater of Dionysus against the southeastern base of the Acropolis. In its initial form, the theater featured an orchestra eighty-five feet in diameter. To avoid another disaster, the seating, which could accommodate up to fourteen thousand spectators, consisted of wooden planking covering earthen tiers carved into the hillside. A rectangular structure called the *skene*, or "scene building," was erected behind the orchestra and facing the audience. The *skene* pro-

vides a background for the actors and also houses dressing rooms and a storage area for stage props.

Various improvements have been made to the theater over the years; but there is still no stone seating, as at the theater at Epidauros (in the Peloponnesus), completed a few years ago by the renowned architect Polyclitus the Younger. (The noted orator Lycurgus promises that if he is given charge of Athens's finances, he will install stone seats in the Theater of Dionysus. His opponents claim this is an empty promise. It will be interesting to see how this political squabble turns out.[24])

Contests, Awards, and Tickets

Despite the existence of theaters in other cities, the dramatic contests held at the

Theater of Dionysus still attract thousands of foreign tourists each year. Most try to take in the whole spectacle from beginning to end. It starts with a splendid procession that winds its way through the urban center and ends in the theater itself. Once the crowd is seated, a bull is sacrificed to Dionysus and the contests begin. Over the course of five days, several playwrights present their works, which are a mix of tragedies and comedies. The comic plays are an important outlet for political expression, since they poke fun, often with amazing candor, at the city's institutions and leaders. Indeed, some visitors say that this demonstration of complete freedom of speech (*parrhesia*) is one of the main factors that draws them to the festival.

Visitors are also drawn by what some see as the festival's most eagerly anticipated moment—the awards ceremony. A panel of ten judges issues lists that rate the work of participants in four categories— tragic playwrights, comic playwrights, leading tragic actors, and leading comic

Two slaves get into mischief behind their master's back in this scene from one of the many popular comedies presented each year at the Theater of Dionysus.

actors. The winner in each category receives a crown of ivy similar to the ones awarded to Olympic victors.

Another thing that invariably impresses visitors is the low admission charge to the theater. A seat for the day costs only two obols, which is very affordable for most people. The tokens look similar to coins and are made of bronze, lead, ivory, bone, or terra-cotta. Impoverished visitors who long to attend the performances can take heart; Athens maintains a special fund that provides theater tickets to the poor. One should apply at the Tholos (the circular structure housing the committee of fifty councillors), in the southwestern sector of the Agora.

Pnyx Hill

Some visitors are intent on seeing the Athenian Assembly, the first completely democratic one in Greece, in action. The Pnyx Hill, site of the Assembly's meetings, is located about 1,200 feet directly west of the Acropolis (with the Areopagus Hill lying between the two). From the southern end of the Acropolis, take the main road west for about 400 feet, make a left turn, and then turn right at the next crossroads. One will then be on the road that leads north to the Potters' Quarter and Market Hill. Walk about 350 feet and some well-worn paths will become visible on the left. These lead up the hill to the Assembly area.

On the slope near the summit, one will see an open amphitheater composed of a stone speaker's platform (*bema*) and a semicircular area with wooden benches for the citizens to sit on. The *bema* originally faced south, standing higher than and looking down on the seats; but about sixty years ago this arrangement was reversed, and today the citizens look down on the platform, which faces north.

Those wishing to watch a meeting should arrive early. Because they are not Athenian citizens, visitors are asked to sit or stand to the rear of the seating section. Also, note that noncitizens are not allowed to ask questions or make proposals; if one wants his concerns aired, he should ask his host or another local citizen to stand and address the Assembly. (On occasion, foreign dignitaries are allowed to speak from the *bema*, but only when invited to do so by a general, councillor, or other public official.)

The Temple of Hephaestos

Another favorite tourist attraction in Athens is the Temple of Hephaestos (or Hephaesteion). It rests on Market Hill, on the northwestern edge of the Agora, in easy view of all points in the northern part of the urban center. From the northwestern corner of the Acropolis, take the Panathenaic Way northward into the Agora. When the Stoa of Zeus becomes visible on the left, walk past the building's left wing and one will see the temple about 150 feet beyond on the slope of the hill.

Though a hexa-style structure and much smaller than the Parthenon, the Hephaesteion is well made and beautiful.

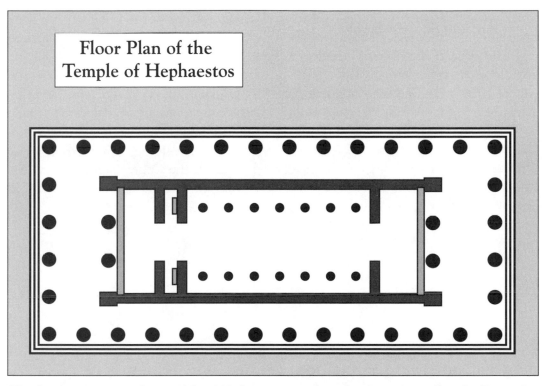

Floor Plan of the
Temple of Hephaestos

The latter measures about 43 by 103 feet and is composed of both Pentelic and Parian marble. Look for the following excellent exterior sculptures: The western pediment shows a scene from the Centauromachy; ten metopes on the east end depict the labors of the famous hero Heracles; and four metopes on each side show various exploits of Theseus. Inside the temple one will find superb bronze cult images of Hephaestos and Athena.

The Stoa Poikile

Perhaps second only to the Parthenon in popularity with tourists is the Stoa Poikile, or "Painted Stoa," in reference to the magnificent paintings displayed there. It is sit-

uated on the Agora's north side. From the Acropolis, follow the Panathenaic Way, as before, until the Stoa of Zeus is visible on your left. The Stoa Poikile lies to the right (east) of the main street, with its front colonnade facing southwest.

Erected in the 450s B.C. by Peisianax, a relative of Cimon's, the Painted Stoa is in a sense a hall of victories. The paintings, done on large wooden boards attached to the masonry walls, all commemorate various renowned battles in which the Athenians took part. The Athenian artist Mikon is responsible for one of the more popular panels, which shows Theseus leading his Athenian troops against the invading Amazons. Another Athenian artist, Panainos (brother of the sculptor Phidias), painted the panel of the Battle of Marathon; and Polygnotos of Thasos did the one depicting scenes from the Trojan War.

The painting of the struggle at Marathon seems to draw the most attention from locals and tourists alike. This no doubt is partly attributable to its heroic theme; but the extraordinary amount of detail supplied by the artist must also be a factor. The faces of the Greek leaders— including Miltiades and Callimachus—are clearly recognizable and must have been copied from busts of these men. Taking some license, the artist also shows the superhuman figures of Theseus, Heracles, and Athena rising from the earth to help the Athenians push back the barbarians, who are seen fleeing toward their ships. This and the other paintings in the Painted Stoa make it a must-see stop in anyone's tour of Athens.[25]

CHAPTER NINE

Daytrips to Nearby Sites

I n addition to the famous sights within Athens's urban center, visitors are
regularly drawn to various spots in surrounding areas of Attica. Some of these
people are religious pilgrims who come to
worship at specific shrines; others are
drawn to the sites of great battles in
which the Athenians repelled barbarian
hordes bent on subjugating all Greeks;
and still others find fascination in the
world-renowned quarries and mines that
produce the marble and silver that make
up so large a proportion of Athens's
wealth. All of the places described below
are within a brisk day's walk of Athens's
urban center and are accessible by pass-
able roads. Local guides are available at
some of the sights for a small fee.

The Acropolis at Eleusis
Eleusis, home of Demeter's shrine and
the Eleusinian Mysteries, is located on
the coast about twelve miles northwest
of the urban center and directly north

of the island of Salamis. The best way
to get there from the urban center is to
go to the Agora and get onto the
Panathenaic Way. Follow this main
road outside the city's walls and contin-
ue westward for about three hours and
the acropolis of Eleusis will become visible in the distance on the left near the
ocean. Travelers coming directly to
Eleusis from western Greece or the
Peloponnesus should take the road that
connects Megara to Eleusis; while those
coming from Boeotia have their own
road that proceeds southward to
Demeter's sanctuary.

Pilgrims who wish to take part in the
great festival of the Mysteries in September will want to go to Athens first,
since the sacred procession begins there, at
the foot of the Acropolis. (On the first day
of the festival, a group of priests journeys
from Eleusis to Athens bearing the sacred
objects and deposits them in the
Eleusinium, Demeter's small temple at the

85

The Propylaea of the acropolis at Eleusis, seen here, is one of the most beautiful in Greece. Demeter's grand temple rises in the distance.

base of the Acropolis. The procession that takes the objects back to Eleusis occurs on the nineteenth of the month.) The procession itself is an experience not to be missed. By custom, the participants shout the names of various gods associated with Demeter; and about halfway to Eleusis, everyone stops and screams obscenities to Iambe, a legendary woman whose own risqué speeches supposedly made Demeter smile. Another highlight of the festival, which takes place after the marchers reach Eleusis, is the reading of the sacred *Homeric Hymn to Demeter*; this ancient text tells the story of how the goddess lost her daughter, Persephone, to the lord of

the Underworld and was later reunited with her.

Whether one takes part in the September festival or simply pays a leisurely visit to Eleusis at another time of the year, he or she is guaranteed to be impressed. The acropolis is one of the two or three most impressive in Greece, next to the one in Athens. One reaches it through a propylaea (gateway) featuring eight massive pillars. Turning left, one finds a smaller gateway that leads to the summit, which is dominated by the Telesterion (great hall of the Mysteries). It is a large, impressive, rectangular structure with a magnificent front porch spanned by twelve columns. Inside, the high ceiling is supported by a veritable forest of pillars. Visitors are allowed inside most of the time but are not allowed to see the sacred objects, which the high priest keeps under lock and key (except during the climax of the great festival).

Another popular sight in Eleusis is the small house in which the great playwright Aeschylus was born. The town has

This drawing represents the goddess Demeter searching for her daughter, Persephone, whom Hades, god of the Underworld, kidnapped and made his queen.

preserved it and almost any local resident can tell the visitor how to find it.

Salamis

Not far south of Eleusis is the island of Salamis, which also lies not far to the northwest of Piraeus. Boats carry supplies to the island from both Eleusis and Piraeus on an irregular basis, and for a small fee they will take travelers across. Fishing boats will also sometimes carry passengers. It is best to check with the dockmaster in each town to find out when the next boat leaves. One can charter a boat, too, but this option is much more expensive.

Salamis has a rich and interesting history. In the Age of Heroes, it was the home of Ajax, one of the greatest Greek warriors who fought at Troy. The locals have set up statues of Ajax and other notable native sons in various parts of the island. In the 600s B.C., three states—Athens, Megara (lying west of Eleusis), and Aegina (the island in the center of the Saronic Gulf, opposite Piraeus)—vied for control of Salamis; and by the middle of the 500s, Athens had taken control of the island.

By far the most important historical event associated with Salamis is the great sea battle fought in its bay, which separates the island from the Attic coast a few miles southwest of Athens's urban center. The conflict took place in 480 B.C., shortly after the Persian king Xerxes had seized Athens (then a mere ghost town, since the inhabitants had recently fled to

Salamis and other nearby locations). From a throne set up on a hill overlooking the bay, the Great King watched the battle, in which his mighty fleet came to death grips with the smaller Greek fleet, commanded by the Athenian general Themistocles. (He claimed overall command because Athens's contingent of two hundred ships was by far the largest in the Greek fleet.)

Xerxes was confident of victory. And, indeed, simple logic dictated that the outnumbered Greeks had no chance. Yet Themistocles and his fellow commanders, knowing that the fate of Greece rested in the balance, found a way to neutralize the enemy's numerical advantage. They hemmed the Persian ships inside the narrow waterway, where these vessels became trapped and had trouble maneuvering. When the Greek fleet attacked, the Persian galleys in the front row slowed almost to a halt; and soon the galleys in the rear rows began piling up on those in the front. This allowed the Greeks to launch ramming runs almost at will. The

An artist has handsomely captured the furious fighting that took place in the Battle of Salamis, fought more than a century ago. Athens led the Greeks to victory.

An Eyewitness to Victory

In his play The Persians, *the Athenian playwright Aeschylus did an excellent job of capturing the atmosphere of the sea battle at Salamis. In this excerpt, a Persian messenger, having returned to the Persian capital of Susa, describes the battle to the Persian queen mother.*

At once ship into ship battered its brazen beak. A Greek ship charged first, and chopped off the whole stern of a Persian galley. Then charge followed charge on every side. At first by its huge impetus our fleet withstood them. But soon, in that narrow space, our ships were jammed in hundreds; none could help another. They rammed each other with their prows of bronze; and some were stripped of every oar. Meanwhile the enemy came round us in a ring and charged. Our vessels heeled over; the sea was hidden, carpeted with wrecks and dead men; all the shores and reefs were full of dead. Then every ship we had broke rank and rowed for life. The Greeks seized fragments of wrecks and broken oars and hacked and stabbed at our men swimming in the sea. . . . The whole sea was one din of shrieks and dying groans, till night and darkness hid the scene.

Athenian playwright Aeschylus, who fought at Salamis, recalled: "At once ship into ship battered its brazen beak. A Greek ship charged first, and chopped off the whole stern of a Persian galley. Then charge followed charge on every side."[26] There was a good deal of hand-to-hand fighting, and Greek sailors and marines slew many enemy seamen struggling in the water. "The Greeks seized fragments of wrecks and broken oars," according to Aeschylus, "and hacked and stabbed at [the Persian] men swimming in the sea."[27] The slaughter was so great and the victory so decisive that no Persian king has dared to attack Greece since that time.

Tourists can view the scene of the battle in a number of ways. Some enjoy hiking to the top of the hill, just to the north of Piraeus, where Xerxes set up his throne to watch the struggle. The exact spot on which he sat is now uncertain. Other visitors prefer to walk along the coast, where rotting timbers from beached Persian galleys are still visible in some places. (Following the battle, thousands of bodies littered the beaches; but these were removed and burned long ago.) Boats can be rented at Piraeus for those who want to dive down in the bay's shallows and try to recover weapons and other artifacts from Persian wrecks.

The Mines at Laurium

To reach Laurium, the site of Athens's renowned silver mines, take the south road from the urban center and travel along the Attic coast. One will pass through the villages of Euonymum, Aexone, Anagyrus, and Anaphlystus. Reaching the latter, take the mining road that heads inland toward the southeast. After four miles or so, the rocky area containing the mines will come into view. The complete journey will take the better part of a day.

The first major strike at the silver mines was in the 490s B.C. Themistocles, who was an archon at the time, convinced the Assembly to spend most of the money on building warships and building new docks at Piraeus to counter a possible Persian threat. Subsequent events proved this to be prudent, of course. Since that time, the Athenian government has run the mines, which have provided untold wealth for the state and its citizens.

Most of the mine workers (*metalleutai*) are slaves. Many foreign visitors are surprised to see the harsh treatment and working conditions endured by these workers, which stand in stark contrast with the situation of other Athenian slaves. Like most Greek slaves, those at Laurium were captured in wars or bought from slave traders and hail from Asia Minor and northern Thrace. Unlike typical Athenian household slaves, who are privately owned, usually well treated, and even frequently become trusted members of the family, the mine slaves are owned by the state. They are often (though not always) criminals or unruly slaves. Furthermore, they are generally shackled day and night, work in stark conditions, and have no hope of gaining their freedom. About thirty-five to forty thousand slaves are at work at Laurium at present. Visitors must be accompanied by a guard at all times and are cautioned not to approach or talk to the slaves.

One can readily see that more than a thousand vertical mine shafts have been drilled into the rocks in the area. They are of varying depths, the deepest being 390 feet. Most measure about six by four feet and have wooden ladders projecting from one wall for the workers to climb up and down. At the bottom of the average shaft, one or more horizontal galleries have been dug along the seams of silver ore. These galleries, in which the miners work lying down on their backs or sides, are from two to three feet high, so needless to say they provide very cramped spaces in which to maneuver. The workers use picks, hammers, and chisels to break loose pieces of ore; then they employ small shovels to load the rocks into baskets. A chain of workers, often young boys, transports the baskets up the shafts to the surface.

After inspecting the mines, some visitors opt to make the four-mile walk northward to the village of Thorikos. The Athenian government recently erected a small theater there, partly for the residents of this and other nearby villages; but hardworking slaves who give the guards no trouble are also allowed to attend. There is no cause to worry, as they remain shackled and guarded at all times.

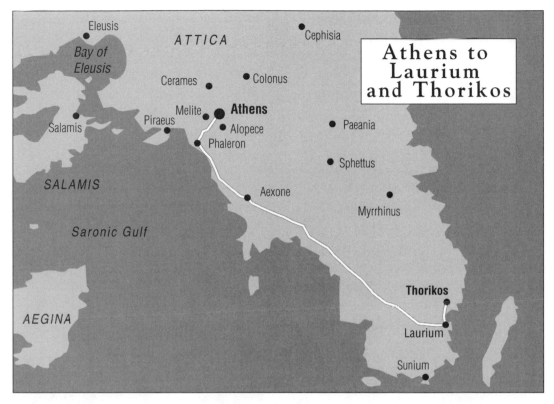

Athens to Laurium and Thorikos

A few guest rooms are available in Thorikos, as well as nearby Anaphlystus. Visitors are urged to get up early in the morning in order to make it back to Athens by sundown.

The Pentelikon Marble Quarries

Another vital and valuable resource for which Athens is well-known, Pentelic marble, has a fine, uniform grain and makes up most of the stones used in the Parthenon and other structures on the Acropolis in the urban center. The marble is quarried on Mount Pentelikon, located about ten miles northeast of Athens. As mentioned earlier in the sec-

tion on roads, the road leading to the quarries is stone-paved and perhaps the best in Greece. At most, the trip takes two and a half hours by foot or donkey.

As there remains a high demand for Pentelic marble throughout the eastern Mediterranean sphere, the quarries are still in operation most of the year. Watching the workers extract the stones from the hillside and transport them to the main road is a fascinating experience, especially for those who have never seen it done. To separate the stones, the quarrymen first use mallets and chisels to cut grooves in the marble. Next, they drive wooden wedges into the grooves and saturate them with water. As the wedges absorb the water, they expand, forcing the stone to crack, after which the workers use crowbars and other tools to finish freeing the stones.

The task of transporting these extremely heavy blocks down the mountainside and across the plain to Athens is daunting, to say the least. Gangs of men use levers, ropes, and pulleys to nudge the stones onto wooden sleds and then, using more ropes, painstakingly maneuver the sleds down the slopes. To help brake the downward momentum of the heaviest stones, the workers set up posts at intervals, each post bearing a block and tackle, out of which runs a rope that is tied to a sled. Despite such safeguards, accidents do happen. On occasion, for instance, the posts or ropes give way, sending a sled plummeting down the hillside. As workers are quick to point out to visitors, a stone intended for one of the Parthenon's columns still rests at the bottom of a nearby ravine.

This drawing captures the extremely difficult job of raising the heavy stones used in constructing a temple. The workers pay heed to the architect, seen at lower right.

Today, a century and a half after the famous battle, the plain of Marathon looks much as it did when a small band of Athenian soldiers saved Greece from foreign conquest.

Once onto the plain, the stones move along the reinforced stone road. The largest blocks require specially made wagons, each with wheels 12 feet in diameter and drawn by up to sixty oxen. To move a single stone from the quarry to the urban center takes at least two days and costs about four hundred drachmas.

The Plain of Marathon

From the Pentelikon quarries it is only about a two- to three-hour walk to one of Attica's major and most exciting tourist sights—the Plain of Marathon. At the end of the paved section near the quarries, the road continues on in the form of an old hill path that leads northeastward and then downhill onto the plain.

The great battle took place in September 490 B.C. Persia's King Darius sent two generals, Datis and Artaphernes, with a large army to destroy Athens and Eretria (on the nearby island of Euboea), because these cities had aided the Ionian rebels in their revolt in the 490s.[28] The Persians managed to capture and burn Eretria (and sold many of its inhabitants into slavery), then made the short journey to the beaches of Marathon, erecting their camp on the eastern edge of the plain. Their initial strategy was apparently to march overland to Athens, some

93

twenty-six miles distant, sack the city, and establish a Persian base in Attica.

To the Persian commanders' surprise, however, an obstacle stood in their path. Athens's entire citizen-militia of some nine thousand hoplites,[29] reinforced by six hundred men from their ally, tiny Plataea, had assembled on the western edge of the plain, blocking the road to Athens. Datis and Artaphernes had little or no idea of the destructive potential of the small army they now faced. They were certainly surprised when the Greeks, despite their greatly inferior numbers, boldly launched a frontal attack on the morning of September 12. The historian Herodotus recalled:

The Persians, seeing the attack developing at the double, prepared to meet it, thinking it suicidal madness for the Athenians to risk an assault with so small a force—rushing in with no support from either cavalry or archers. . . . Nevertheless, the Athenians came on, closed with the enemy . . . and fought in a way not to be forgotten.[30]

Indeed, in the bloody battle that followed, the Greek soldiers proved more disciplined and far deadlier than the Persian troops, who eventually fell back and fled in confusion to the nearby swamps and beaches. The Greeks gave chase and managed to capture seven ships before the fleet escaped. Datis and Artaphernes, having lost over sixty-four hundred men, soon aborted their mission.

Supernatural Events at Marathon

Marathon was and remains a mysterious place of miraculous and supernatural happenings. Not only do some people say that they hear the ghosts of soldiers haunting the battlefield, but stories persist that Theseus, Herakles, and other ancient heroes rose up to aid the Athenians during the struggle. Also, the historian Herodotus told this chilling story in his Histories:

During the action, a very strange thing happened: Epizelus . . . an Athenian soldier, was fighting bravely when he suddenly lost the sight of both eyes, though nothing had touched him anywhere—neither sword, spear, nor missile. From that moment, he continued blind as long as he lived. I am told that when speaking about what happened to him, he used to say that he fancied he was opposed by a man of great stature in heavy armor, whose beard overshadowed his shield; but the phantom passed him by, and killed the man at his side.

Only 192 Athenians were killed in the struggle. Under normal circumstances, they would have been transported back to the city, cremated, and buried in the cemetery lying outside the Thriasian Gate. But to commemorate their heroic sacrifice, which filled Greeks everywhere with pride, the state cremated and buried them right there on the plain. The mound covering their bodies is still visible.[31] It and the plain itself never fail to elicit in visitors genuine feelings of emotion, even awe. Indeed, many claim that at night they can hear faint but distinct sounds of men fighting and dying.

Visitors desiring to stay overnight in the area can find guest rooms in the small village of Marathon, which lies slightly over a mile north of the battlefield. Even there, the spirits of Greeks long dead are said to appear from time to time. Such eerie events remind us all that the present has been shaped and remains linked to the past by the deeds of our illustrious ancestors.

Notes

Chapter One: A Brief History of Athens

1. The late Greek Bronze Age, dated by historians to circa 1500–1100 B.C.
2. Herodotus, *The Histories*, trans. Aubrey de Sélincourt. New York: Penguin, 1972, p. 364.
3. Demosthenes, *Second Philippic*, in *Olynthiacs, Philippics, Minor Speeches*, trans. J.H. Vince. Cambridge, MA: Harvard University Press, 1962, pp. 141–43.

Chapter Two: Weather and Physical Setting

4. What is now western Turkey, where numerous Greek cities were located in ancient times.
5. This is slightly larger than the state of Rhode Island.
6. Plato, *Critias*, in *The Dialogues of Plato*, trans. Benjamin Jowett. Chicago: Encyclopaedia Britannica, 1952, p. 480.
7. Called the Dipylon Gate after about 280 B.C.

Chapter Three: Transportation, Lodging, and Food

8. Quoted in James Davidson, *Courtesans and Fishcakes: The Consuming Passions of Classical Athens*. New York: St. Martin's Press, 1998, p. 54.

9. Quoted in Davidson, *Courtesans and Fishcakes*, p. 42.

Chapter Four: Shopping

10. What is now France.
11. Today called Elba.

Chapter Five: Athenian Government

12. Plato, *Laws*, in *Dialogues of Plato*, p. 676.
13. Warships with three banks (levels) of oars.

Chapter Six: Religious Worship and Festivals

14. One of the sculptures on the Parthenon shows this folding ceremony. For it and more on the *peplos*, see Ian Jenkins, *The Parthenon Frieze*. Austin: University of Texas, 1994, pp. 24–26, 29–30, 35–42, 79.

Chapter Seven: Athletics and Recreation

15. Quoted in Waldo E. Sweet, ed., *Sport and Recreation in Ancient Greece: A Sourcebook with Translations*. New York: Oxford University Press, 1987, p. 120.
16. Lower leg protectors, usually made of bronze.

17. Sophocles, *Electra*, in *Electra and Other Plays*, trans. E.F. Watling. Baltimore: Penguin, 1953, p. 90.
18. Plato, *Laws*, in *Dialogues of Plato*, p. 726.
19. Modern scholars are uncertain about the particulars but believe it was similar to modern rugby.

Chapter Eight: Sightseeing in Athens

20. In this myth, Philoctetes was a Greek warrior stranded on Lemnos, and Odysseus had to rescue him to fulfill a prophecy and ensure a Greek victory in the Trojan War.
21. In the well-known myth of the Curse of the House of Atreus, Orestes, a prince of Mycenae, sought revenge on Aegisthus, who had murdered Orestes' father, Agamemnon.
22. Today the original Karyatids are in museums to protect them from further deterioration, and the statues visible on the south porch are replicas.
23. Quoted in Thucydides, *The Peloponnesian War*, trans. Rex Warner. New York: Penguin, 1972, p. 148.
24. Lycurgus kept his promise. Between 338 and 325 B.C., he overhauled the theater and added stone seats.
25. Shortly after 300 B.C., the Stoa Poikile lent its name to a new philosophical movement—Stoicism—because its founder, Zeno, often lectured there.

Chapter Nine: Daytrips to Nearby Sites

26. Aeschylus, *The Persians*, in *Prometheus Bound, The Suppliants, Seven Against Thebes, The Persians*, trans. Philip Vellacott. Baltimore: Penguin Books, 1961, p. 134.
27. Aeschylus, *Persians*, p. 134.
28. The Ionian Greek cities rebelled against Persia in 499 B.C. but were defeated and recaptured by 494. Athens and Eretria sent ships and men to help the Ionians, which angered Darius.
29. Heavily armored infantry soldiers who fought with thrusting spears and bronze swords.
30. Herodotus, *Histories*, p. 429.
31. The mound is still intact today. Modern archaeologists excavated it but out of respect they left the heroes' remains in place.

For Further Reading

Isaac Asimov, *The Greeks: A Great Adventure*. Boston: Houghton Mifflin, 1965. An excellent, entertaining overview of Greek history and culture.

David Bellingham, *An Introduction to Greek Mythology*. Secaucus, NJ: Chartwell Books, 1989. Explains the major Greek myths and legends and their importance to the ancient Greeks. Contains many beautiful photos and drawings.

C.M. Bowra, *Classical Greece*. New York: Time-Life, 1965. Despite the passage of more than thirty years, this volume—written by a renowned classical historian and adorned with numerous maps, drawings, and color photos—is only slightly dated and remains one of the best introductions to ancient Greece for general readers.

Denise Dersin, *Greece: Temples, Tombs, and Treasures*. Alexandria, VA: Time-Life, 1994. In a way a newer companion volume to Bowra's book (see above), this is also excellent and features a long, up-to-date, and beautifully illustrated chapter on Athens's Golden Age.

Rhoda A. Hendricks, trans., *Classical Gods and Heroes*. New York: Morrow Quill, 1974. A collection of easy-to-read translations of famous Greek myths and tales, as told by ancient Greek and Roman writers, including Homer, Hesiod, Pindar, Apollodorus, Ovid, and Virgil.

Susan Peach and Anne Millard, *The Greeks*. London: Usborne, 1990. A general overview of the history, culture, myths, and everyday life of ancient Greece, presented in a format suitable to young, basic readers (although the many fine, accurate color illustrations make the book appealing to anyone interested in ancient Greece).

Jonathon Rutland, *See Inside an Ancient Greek Town*. New York: Barnes and Noble, 1995. This colorful introduction to ancient Greek life is aimed at basic readers.

Don Nardo, *The Age of Pericles*. San Diego: Lucent Books, 1996.

———, *The Battle of Marathon*. San Diego: Lucent Books, 1996.

———, *Greek and Roman Sport*. San Diego: Lucent Books, 1999.

————, *Greek and Roman Theater*. San Diego: Lucent Books, 1995.

————, *Leaders of Ancient Greece*. San Diego: Lucent Books, 1999.

————, *Life in Ancient Greece*. San Diego: Lucent Books, 1996.

————, *The Parthenon*. San Diego: Lucent Books, 1999.

————, *Scientists of Ancient Greece*. San Diego: Lucent Books, 1998.

————, *The Trial of Socrates*. San Diego: Lucent Books, 1997.

Major Works Consulted

Modern Sources

Lesly Adkins and Roy A. Adkins, *Handbook to Life in Ancient Greece*. New York: Facts on File, 1997. A fulsome compilation of useful facts about ancient Greek history, culture, and people.

Manolis Andronicos, *The Acropolis*. Athens: Ekdotike Athenon, 1994. This terrific guide to the monuments on Athens's Acropolis was written by one of Greece's finest modern scholars and is highly recommended.

James H. Butler, *The Theater and Drama of Greece and Rome*. San Francisco: Chandler Publishing, 1972. An excellent summary of ancient theaters, actors, playwrights, and play production.

Lionel Casson, *Travel in the Ancient World*. Baltimore: Johns Hopkins University Press, 1994. The author of one modern classic, *The Ancient Mariners*, has produced another instant classic—a readable, highly authoritative work filled with valuable information and insights about a topic few other modern scholars approach in any detail.

David Cohen, *Law, Violence, and Community in Classical Athens*. New York: Cambridge University Press, 1995. A somewhat scholarly, very well-written, and well-documented account of some important aspects of ancient Athenian society.

James Davidson, *Courtesans and Fishcakes: The Consuming Passions of Classical Athens*. New York: St. Martin's Press, 1998. This scholarly book manages to seem nonscholarly, partly because it deals with society's vices (wine drinking, cooking, gluttony, prostitution, and so on) and also because of the author's sense of humor.

N.R.E. Fisher, *Social Values in Classical Athens*. London: Dent, 1976. One of the best general overviews of ancient Greek society, social values, and social status available.

Mark Golden, *Children and Childhood in Classical Athens*. Baltimore: Johns Hopkins University Press, 1990. This will be difficult reading for young people and nonbuffs of ancient times, but it is a thorough, well-informed study of the topic.

Peter Green, *The Parthenon*. New York: Newsweek Book Division, 1973. A very handsomely illustrated presentation of ancient Athens, emphasizing the buildings on the Acropolis and when and how they were built, but discussing many other aspects of Athenian society as well.

Joint Association of Classical Teachers, *The World of Athens: An Introduction to Classical Athenian Culture*. New York: Cambridge University Press, 1984. An extremely thorough overview of ancient Athenian society compiled by a group of professors who teach classics on a regular basis. Also valuable for its inclusion of hundreds of transliterated Greek words.

Malcolm F. McGregor, *The Athenians and Their Empire*. Vancouver: University of British Columbia Press, 1987. One of the best overviews available of the political and economic aspects of Athens in the Classical Age.

Christian Meier, *Athens: Portrait of a City in Its Golden Age*. Trans. Robert and Rita Kimber. New York: Henry Holt, 1998. A widely acclaimed synopsis of Athens in the Classical Age.

Evi Melas, *Temples and Sanctuaries of Ancient Greece*. London: Thames and Hudson, 1973. Melas discusses the major temples and religious sights of ancient Greece one by one, providing information about their construction, uses, and importance. A valuable book.

John D. Mikalson, *Athenian Popular Religion*. Chapel Hill: University of North Carolina Press, 1983. A thorough overview of Athenian religion, including information about sacrifices and other rituals, funeral customs, beliefs about the afterlife, and much more.

Jennifer Neils, *Goddess and Polis: The Panathenaic Festival in Ancient Athens*. Princeton, NJ: Princeton University Press, 1992. The definitive study of Athens's most important religious festival. Highly recommended.

Vera Olivova, *Sports and Games in the Ancient World*. New York: St. Martin's Press, 1984. Well written and entertaining, this book covers the panorama of ancient sports, including Greek athletic games, in considerable detail.

R.E. Wycherly, *The Stones of Athens*. Princeton, NJ: Princeton University Press, 1978. One of the few books, and perhaps the best, that attempts to catalog and describe in some detail all of the major (and many of the minor) buildings and sights in ancient Athens as revealed by modern archaeology. A very valuable book.

Ancient Sources

Aeschylus, *The Persians*, in *Aeschylus: Prometheus Bound, The Suppliants, Seven Against Thebes, The Persians*. Trans. Philip Vellacott. Baltimore: Penguin, 1961; and the *Oresteia*, published as *The Orestes Plays of Aeschylus*. Trans. Paul Roche. New York: New American Library, 1962.

Aristophanes, *The Complete Plays of Aristophanes*. Ed. Moses Hadas. New York: Bantam, 1962.

Aristotle, *The Athenian Constitution*. Trans. H. Rackham. 1952. Reprint, Cambridge, MA: Harvard University Press, 1996.

Kenneth J. Atchity, ed., *The Classical Greek Reader*. New York: Oxford University Press, 1996. A collection of translations of ancient Greek writings, including those of Homer, Solon, Herodotus, Lysias, Xenophon, Aristotle, Sophocles, Demosthenes, and many others.

Demosthenes, *Olynthiacs, Philippics, Minor Speeches*. Trans. J.H. Vince. Cambridge, MA: Harvard University Press, 1962.

Herodotus, *The Histories*. Trans. Aubrey de Sélincourt. New York: Penguin, 1972.

Hesiod, *Theogony*, in *Hesiod and Theognis*. Trans. Dorothea Wender. New York: Penguin, 1973.

Pausanias, *Guide to Greece*. 2 vols. Trans. Peter Levi. New York: Penguin, 1971.

Pindar, *Odes*. Trans. C.M. Bowra. New York: Penguin, 1969.

Plato, *Dialogues*, in *The Dialogues of Plato*. Trans. Benjamin Jowett. Chicago: Encyclopaedia Britannica, 1952.

Plutarch, *Parallel Lives*, excerpted in *The Rise and Fall of Athens: Nine Greek Lives by Plutarch*. Trans. Ian Scott-Kilvert. New York: Penguin, 1960. Includes the *Life of Solon*, which contains poetry attributed to Solon himself.

J.J. Pollitt, ed. and trans., *The Art of Ancient Greece: Sources and Documents*. New York: Cambridge University Press, 1990. A compilation of translations of ancient sources dealing with painting, sculpture, architecture, and other artistic genres.

Sophocles, *Electra and Other Plays*. Trans. E.F. Watling. Baltimore: Penguin, 1953.

———, *Oedipus the King*. Trans. Bernard M.W. Knox. New York: Pocket Books, 1959.

Waldo E. Sweet, ed., *Sport and Recreation in Ancient Greece: A Sourcebook with Translations*. New York: Oxford University Press, 1987. A collection of translations of ancient sources describing sports, games, music, dance, theater, and related leisure activities.

Theophrastus, *Characters*. Trans. Jeffrey Rustin. Cambridge, MA: Harvard University Press, 1993.

Thucydides, *The Peloponnesian War*. Trans. Rex Warner. New York: Penguin, 1972; and also published as *The Landmark Thucydides: A Comprehensive Guide to the Peloponnesian War*. Trans. Richard Crawley, ed. Robert B. Strassler. New York: Simon & Schuster, 1996.

Thomas Wiedemann, ed., *Greek and Roman Slavery*. Baltimore: Johns Hopkins University Press, 1981. A compilation of translations of ancient sources dealing with slavery.

Xenophon, *Anabasis*. Trans. W.H.D. Rouse. New York: New American Library, 1959.

———, *Hellenica*, published as *A History of My Times*. Trans. Rex Warner. New York: Penguin, 1979.

———, *Memorabilia and Oeconomicus*. Trans. E.C. Marchant. Cambridge, MA: Harvard University Press, 1965.

———, *Scripta Minora*. Trans. E.C. Marchant. Cambridge, MA: Harvard University Press, 1993.

Additional Works Consulted

H.C. Baldry, *The Greek Tragic Theater*. New York: W.W. Norton, 1971.

Carl Bluemel, *Greek Sculptors at Work*. London: Phaidon, 1969.

Sue Blundell, *Women in Ancient Greece*. Cambridge, MA: Harvard University Press, 1995.

John Boardman, ed., *The Oxford History of Classical Art*. Oxford: Oxford University Press, 1993.

———, *The Parthenon and Its Sculptures*. Austin: University of Texas, 1985.

C.M. Bowra, *Periclean Athens*. New York: Dial Press, 1971.

Walter Burkert, *Greek Religion, Archaic and Classical*. Oxford: Basil Blackwell, 1985.

Lionel Casson, *Masters of Ancient Comedy*. New York: Macmillan, 1960.

Peter Connolly, *Greece and Rome at War*. London: Greenhill Books, 1998.

Thomas Craven, *The Pocket Book of Greek Art*. New York: Pocket Books, 1950.

J.K. Davies, *Democracy and Classical Greece*. Cambridge, MA: Harvard University Press, 1993.

M.I. Finley and H.W. Pleket, *The Olympic Games: The First Thousand Years*. New York: Viking Press, 1976.

Kathleen Freeman, *The Murder of Herodes and Other Trials from the Athenian Law Courts*. New York: W.W. Norton, 1963.

Robert Garland, *The Greek Way of Life*. Ithaca, NY: Cornell University Press, 1990.

Michael Grant, *Greek and Roman Historians: Information and Misinformation*. London: Routledge, 1995.

———, *Guide to the Ancient World*. New York: Barnes and Noble, 1996.

———, *The Rise of the Greeks*. New York: Macmillan, 1987.

Peter Green, *The Greco-Persian Wars*. Berkeley: University of California Press, 1996.

Victor D. Hanson, *The Western Way of War: Infantry Battle in Classical Greece*. New York: Oxford University Press, 1989.

Ian Jenkins, *The Parthenon Frieze*. Austin: University of Texas, 1994.

Robert B. Kebric, *Greek People*. Mountain View, CA: Mayfield Publishing, 2001.

A.W. Lawrence, rev. R.A. Tomlinson, *Greek Architecture*. New Haven, CT: Yale University Press, 1996.

Peter Levi, *Atlas of the Greek World*. New York: Facts On File, 1984.

Douglas M. MacDowell, *The Law in Classical Athens*. Ithaca, NY: Cornell University Press, 1978.

Thomas R. Martin, *Ancient Greece: From Prehistoric to Hellenistic Times*. New Haven, CT: Yale University Press, 1996.

John Miliadis, *The Acropolis*. Athens: M. Pechlivanidis, n.d.

Sarah B. Pomeroy, *Goddesses, Whores, Wives, and Slaves: Women in Classical Antiquity*. New York: Schocken Books, 1995.

C.A. Robinson, *Athens in the Age of Pericles*. Norman: University of Oklahoma, 1971.

C.E. Robinson, *Everyday Life in Ancient Greece*. Oxford: Clarendon Press, 1968.

Eli Sagan, *The Honey and the Hemlock: Democracy and Paranoia in Ancient Athens and Modern America*. New York: HarperCollins, 1991.

Erika Simon, *Festivals of Attica: An Archaeological Commentary*. Madison: University of Wisconsin Press, 1983.

Nigel Spivey, *Greek Art*. London: Phaidon, 1997.

Chester G. Starr, *A History of the Ancient World*. New York: Oxford University Press, 1991.

Judith Swaddling, *The Ancient Olympic Games*. Austin: University of Texas Press, 1980, 1996.

Richard J.A. Talbert, ed., *Atlas of Classical History*. London: Routledge, 1985.

Panayotis Tournikiotis, ed., *The Parthenon and Its Impact in Modern Times*. New York: Harry N. Abrams, 1996.

George D. Wilcoxon, *Athens Ascendant*. Ames: Iowa State University Press, 1979.

Alfred Zimmern, *The Greek Commonwealth: Politics and Economics in Fifth-Century Athens*. 5th ed. New York: Oxford University Press, 1931. Revised and reprinted, 1961.

Index

Academy, 71
accommodations, 27–30
Acropolis, 10 (illus.), 11, 22 (illus.),
   72 (illus.)
   creation of, 15
   described, 72–75
   Parthenon, 75–78
   plan of, 73
aegis, 11
Aeschines, 16
Aeschylus, 60, 87, 89
Age of Heroes, 10, 11
Agora, 22 (illus.), 23, 30, 34 (illus.),
   37–38, 45 (illus.), 72
agriculture, 20–21
Ajax, 87
altars, 75
Amazons, 11, 76, 78
animal sacrifices, 58–59
Anthesteria, 59
apobates, 68
Apollo (god), 52
archons, 46
Areopagus, 22, 46
Ares (god), 52
Artemis (goddess), 52, 74
artisans, 38–41
Assembly (Ecclesia), 12, 13, 43–44, 82
Athena (goddess)
   about, 52
   Athens and, 53–56

birth of, 11
   Panathenaea and, 56–59
   sacred robe of, 57–59
Athena Nike, 55
Athena Parthenos, 54, 78
Athena Polias, 56
Athena Promachos, 54–55, 55
   (photo), 73, 74
Athens, layout of, 22–23
athletes/athletics, 62–71
   female, 68
   glorification of, 62–63
   gymnasia, 70–71
   physical training for, 70–71
   rewards for, 64–65
athletic competitions
   Heraea, 68
   Olympics, 63–64, 68
   Panathenaic Games, 64–69
   tribal contests, 68–70
atimos, 44
Attica, 11
   geography of, 18–21
   map of, 20, 24

bankers, 26–27, 36
bathhouses, 29–30
Battle of Marathon, 84, 93–95
Battle of Salamis, 87–89
Bouphonia, 60–61
bronze works, 41

calendar, 53
Cecrops (king), 11
Centaurs, 76
ceramics, 39–41
Chalcotheca, 74
chariot races, 67–68
Chian wine, 32–33
choregus, 80
Cimon, 15
citizens' rights, 43–44, 48
City Dionysia, 61, 79
Classical Age, 8
clay, 19
Cleisthenes, 13
climate, 18
coins, 35 (photo), 35–36
Council (Boule), 13, 44–46
courts, 48–50
cuisine, 30–32
currency, 35–36

Darius I (king), 14
dating systems, 8
Delphic oracle, 53, 54 (illus.)
demes, 42
Demeter (goddess), 59–60, 86
democracy, 12–14, 42–43
  see also government, institutions
Democratia, 61
demos, 42
Demosthenes, 16 (illus.), 16–17, 48
Diogenes the Cynic, 31
Dionysus (god), 32, 59
Dipolieia, 60–61
Doric frieze, 76
Draco, 12
dramatic competitions, 79, 80–82

Ecclesia (Assembly), 12, 13, 43–44, 82

Electra (Sophocles), 67–68
Eleusinian Mysteries, 59–60
Eleusis, 85–87
Epaminondas, 15
episkyros, 71
equestrian races, 67–68
Erechtheum, 56, 74 (illus.), 74–75

festivals. *See individual festival names*
First Philippic (Demosthenes), 16
food, 30–32
footraces, 65–66

generals, 46–47
geography, 18–21
Gigantomachy, 76–77, 78
gods and goddesses
  overview of, 51–53
  see also individual names of gods and
    goddesses
government, 42
  growth of democracy, 12–14
  institutions
    Assembly, 43–44
    citizenship and, 43–44, 48
    Council, 44–46
    courts, 48–50
    strategia, 46–47
  see also democracy
Greater Panathenaea, 56–59
Greece, map of, 19
gymnasia, 62, 70–71

Helen (queen), 11
Hephaesteion, 82–83
Hephaestos (god), 52
Hera (goddess), 51
Heraea, 68
hermeia, 29

Hermes (god), 29
Hermippus, 32–33
Herodotus, 13, 94
Hesiod (poet), 11
Hippodamus, 23
history, 10–17
  Age of Heroes, 11
  growth of democracy, 12–14
  Peloponnesian War, 15, 21
  threat from Macedonians, 16–17
  war with Persians, 14, 93–95
Homer, 11, 12
Homeric Hymn to Demeter, 86
hoplitodromos, 65–66, 66 (illus.)
horse races, 67–68
hospitality, 27
houses, 27
hunting, 71

Ictinus, 75
Iliad (Homer), 11, 12
imports, 35
Industrial District, 38–39
inns, 28–29
Ionic frieze, 77

justice system, 43, 48–50

kalokagathia, 62–63
Kerameikos, 39
Lapiths, 76
Laurium, 89–91
law, equality under, 13–14
laws, 12
Leuctra, 15
liturgies, 80
loans, 36
lodging, 27–30

Macedonians, 16–17
maps
  Attica, 20, 24
  Greece, 19
  Laurium and Thorikos, 91
Marathon, Battle of, 93–95
marble, 19, 91–93
measurements, 8–9
merchants, 37–41
metalsmiths, 41
metics, 44
Metis (goddess), 11
metopes, 76–77
Mikon, 83
military leaders, 46–47
mines, Laurium, 89–91
Mithaecus, 33
monetary system, 36
money, 35–36, 38
monuments
  Athena Promachos, 54–55, 55
    (photo), 73, 74
    Doric frieze, 76
    Parthenon, 53–54, 75 (illus.), 75–78
Mount Pentelikon, 91

natural resources, 19

Odyssey (Homer), 12
Oedipus the King (Sophocles), 25
Olympics, 63–64, 68
Olynthiacs (Demosthenes), 16
oracles, 53
ostracism, 47

Painted Stoa, 83–84
palaestrae, 71
Panainos, 83–84

Panathenaea, 51, 56–59
Panathenaic Games, 64
  combat events, 66
  equestrian races, 67–68
  footraces, 65–66
  pentathlon, 66
  tribal contests, 68–69
pankration, 66
Paris, 11
Parthenon, 53–54, 75 (illus.), 75–78
Peisianax, 83
Peloponnesian War, 15, 21
Peloponnesus, 15
pentathlon, 66
Pentelic marble, 91–93
peplos, 57–59
Pericles, 15 (illus.), 47 (illus.), 73
Persephone, 86, 87
Persians, 14, 93–95
Persians, The (Aeschylus), 89
Phidias, 52, 73, 75, 78
Phillip II (king), 8, 16–17
physical setting, 18–21
physical training, 70–71
Piraeus, 17, 21 (illus.), 23
Plain of Marathon, 93 (illus.), 93–95
Plato, 20, 42–43, 69, 71
Pnyx Hill, 22–23, 82
Polygnotos of Thasos, 84
Porch of the Maidens, 74 (illus.), 75
Poseidon (god), 11, 51–52
pottery, 19, 39–41
prayer, 52
prices, 38
priests, 52–53
Propylaea, 73–74, 86 (illus.)
proxenos, 26

public officials, 46–47
Pyrrhic dance, 69

races
  chariot, 67–68
  foot, 65–66
  horse, 67–68
  torch, 69–70
religious festivals. See religious rituals; names of individual festivals
religious rituals
  for Athena, 53–56
  basics of, 51–53
  gods and goddesses, 51–56
  importance of, 51
  prayer, 52
  sacrifices, 58–59, 61
roads, 25–26
robbers, 25, 26–27
runners, 65–66

sacrifices, 58–59, 61
Salamis, 14, 87–89
Sarambus, 33
sea travel, 24–25
shops, 37–41
silver mines, 89–91
slaves, 37, 44, 90
Socrates, 49 (illus.)
Solon, 12–13, 14 (illus.)
Sophocles, 25, 67–68
Sparta, 15–16
sports. See athletes/athletics
Stoa Poikile, 83–84
strategia, 46–47
symposia, 32
Synoecia, 61

taverns, 31–32
Telesterion, 86–87
temples
  Athena Nike, 73
  Erechtheum, 74–75
  Hephaestos, 82–83
  Parthenon, 53–54, 75 (illus.),
    75–78
terrain, 18–21
Theater of Dionysus, 79–82
Themistocles, 14, 88, 90
Theogamia, 61
Theogony (Hesiod), 11
Theseus, 11
Thesmophoria, 60
Thorikos, 90–91
Thriasian Gate, 22 (illus.), 23
torches, 31
torch races, 69–70

trade, 21, 34–35
transportation, 24–27
tribal contests, 68–70
Trojan Horse, 13 (illus.)
Trojan War, 77
Troy, 11
Truce-bearers, 63

voting rights, 44, 48

wages, 38
weather, 18
wines, 32–33
women, 38, 44, 48
wrestling training, 71

Xerxes (king), 14, 73, 87–88

Zeus (god), 11, 51, 52 (illus.)

Picture Credits

Cover photo: Leeds Museums and Galleries (City Art Gallery)
U.K./Bridgeman Art Library

© Archivo Iconographico, S.A./CORBIS, 35

© Bettmann/CORBIS, 14, 15, 34, 37, 43, 92

Dover Publications, Inc., 54, 56

© Hulton/Archive by Getty Images, 47

Chris Jouan, 19, 20, 24, 73, 76, 79, 83, 91

Bob Kebric, 93

© Erich Lessing/Art Resource, NY, 39, 61

Library of Congress, 49

Mary Evans Picture Library, 87

© Massimo Listri/CORBIS, 67

© North Wind Pictures, 10, 21, 22, 27, 28, 30, 32, 45, 58–59, 63, 66, 70, 74, 75, 78, 81, 86

© Gianni Dagli Orti/CORBIS, 72

© Réunion des Musées Nationaux/Art Resource, NY, 40

© Ted Spiegel/CORBIS, 77

© Stock Montage, Inc., 13, 16, 29, 52, 55, 64, 69, 88

About the Author

Historian Don Nardo has written numerous volumes about the ancient Greek world, including *The Age of Pericles*, *Greek and Roman Sport*, *The Parthenon*, and *The Greenhaven Encyclopedia of Greek and Roman Mythology*. He is also the editor of Greenhaven's *Complete History of Ancient Greece* and literary companions to the works of Homer and Sophocles. Along with his wife, Christine, he resides in Massachusetts.